W9-BRK-375

2614

New
Teachers
in
Urban Schools

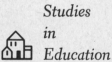

*Studies
in
Education*

Consulting Editor: PAUL NASH

RANDOM HOUSE: New York

New
Teachers
in
Urban Schools:
An
Inside
View

Richard Wisniewski   WAYNE STATE
UNIVERSITY

LC5131.W5   ST. JOSEPH'S UNIVERSITY   STX
New teachers in urban schools:

3 9353 00145 3552

151363

LC
5131
.W5

9 8 7 6 5 4 3 2

© Copyright, 1968, by Random House,
Inc.

All rights reserved under International
and Pan-American Copyright Conventions. Published in New York by Random House, Inc. and simultaneously
in Toronto, Canada, by Random House
of Canada Limited.

Library of Congress Catalog Card
Number: 68–13169

Manufactured in the United States of
America

Typography by Leon Bolognese

For
Britt-Mari

Preface

This book is essentially a personal document. The ideas suggested in it are based on fifteen years of teaching experience, ranging from the elementary grades to the graduate school. All but one of these years have been spent in an urban setting. More recently, my work as an educational sociologist has been focused on the problems of educating disadvantaged youth. With others, I have been forced to the conclusion that many of these problems are accentuated by the rigidity of many teachers, schools, and school systems. Not that reform efforts are lacking. On the contrary, American education has been said to be in ferment, and programs designed for the disadvantaged child are much in evidence. I am convinced that the ultimate test of public education is the degree to which schools meet or fail to meet the challenges of urban life. Efforts to "reach" disadvantaged youth more effectively are therefore viewed both hopefully and skeptically. As long as most of the reforms are restricted to pilot and demonstration projects, much limited in scope and impact, I am not at all confident that most school systems are capable of meeting the problems of our times.

This statement does not mean, however, that the views expressed here are either pessimistic or negative. Teaching conditions in inner-city schools are not outlined in sensational terms. Neither teachers nor school systems are solely responsible for problems and issues that no one segment of society can solve. On the other hand, every teacher in an urban school system can contribute either to the modification or the continuation of premises, practices, and prejudices that *are* the responsibilities of teachers and schools. And the fulfillment of some of these responsibilities is clearly in need of drastic reform.

As our focus is on many of the restrictive aspects of becoming part of a major school system, it should be stressed that criticism and rejection are not necessarily the same. Perhaps an anecdote will make this point clear. Some years ago, I recall a professor being challenged in class because, in the process of contrasting the Italian and American cultures, he would often cite inequities and dysfunctions in the American culture. A student asked didn't the professor "like anything" about the United States. The professor replied that he criticized the United States because he loved it. He knew the potential for greatness within his country, and he had to speak forth on ways he thought this potential could indeed be achieved. This answer has remained with me. My feeling toward school systems is very much the same.

I feel no need to expound at length on the strengths and tremendous potential of the free public-education system as it has evolved in the United States. It is because I am wholly committed to the promises of that system that I am compelled to be critical of it. More than one teacher or administrator has raised the question "Don't we do anything right?" when discussions focus on the problems of urban education. The only answer I can offer is that an excellent rationale has been developed by many writers dealing with the virtues of American education. But the problems facing the urban schools are tremendous, and there seems little point to waxing eloquent about what we have done. We are far more concerned with the dysfunctions of the system and ways to improve it. The need for reform in education has long been with us, but efforts to achieve it have borne little fruit. And we are in the process of losing still another generation while we either laud the past, rationalize the present, or ignore the future.

In short, this work is not an exposé. There are no villains and no scapegoats. I have attempted to sketch a portrait of certain aspects of teaching that will be familiar to many experienced teachers but that are likely to be unknown or poorly understood by the newcomer to teaching. Some of the ideas discussed here may indeed discourage some young people from entering the profession. If they have any commitment whatever to the broader goals of American democracy and of public education, then I do not believe this will be the result. If they do not have such a commitment, it is unlikely that any book is going to develop it.

This effort is at best an introduction to teaching in general and to teaching in urban schools in particular. If it is directed toward any one group, it is toward college students engaged in teacher-education programs. Hopefully, it is a candid analysis of some of the facts of life in city school systems. It is also an attempt to clarify some of the misconceptions regarding teaching in disadvantaged areas, though it is not focused exclusively on inner-city schools. Most important, it is an attempt to provide a frame of reference for people who wish to continue their own investigations of "life in the trenches."

I am indebted to several friends, colleagues, and students who have shared their experiences in urban schools with me. My sincere thanks go to the following individuals, each of whom has contributed materials reproduced in Chapters 4 and 5: Miss Sandra Acker, a former student, who is currently doing advanced work in the sociology of education; Miss Miriam Dann, a teacher of English in an inner-city high school; Miss Susan Dubrinsky, also a former student and now an elementary-school teacher; Mrs. Erlene Flowers, an art teacher in an inner-city junior high school; Dr. Freeman Flynn, principal of an inner-city junior high school and involved in many efforts to improve urban education; Dr. Arnold Glovinsky, a former teacher and department head, now the director of a study to determine appropriate tasks for paraprofessionals in public schools; Mrs. Hazel Karbel, a teacher in an inner-city junior high school; and Miss Donna Schwab, who taught for one year in an inner-city high school and is now doing advanced work in her field. I am also grateful for permission to reprint Miss Dann's article from the May–June 1966 issue of *Now!*

These people are in no sense responsible for the points of view expressed here. Their contributions represent the insights of, hopefully, a growing number of competent inner-city teachers and administrators. Each of them offers ideas of particular relevance to people who have yet to enter "the system."

Detroit, 1968   **Richard Wisniewski**

Contents

New
Teachers
in
Urban Schools

Chapter 1

Introduction

In recent years, the disadvantaged child and inner-city schools have become major topics of discussion among educators, sociologists, social workers, and people developing the antipoverty program. As Michael Harrington's book *The Other America* has helped to make clear, extensive poverty and life styles within the subculture of poverty are hardly new phenomena.[1] Poverty and prejudice have long been part of our society. Yet it is only recently that scholarly and popular attention has been focused on the many problems related to economic, social, and psychological deprivation, particularly as they relate to education. Since about 1960, for example, symposia and lectures on the disadvantaged child have become part of virtually every national convention of teachers, school administrators, and teacher educators. If conventions and other types of meetings or workshops are effective in transmitting knowledge, the teaching profession has indeed been exposed to a wide range of analyses, exhortations, and suggestions related to the educational needs of disadvantaged youth.

It is sometimes suggested that the disadvantaged have pricked the national conscience because of the glaring disparities between poverty and affluence in our society. It is probably more accurate to state that the concentration of low-income families in minority-group ghettos in our cities and the white middle-class exodus to the suburbs over the last twenty years are more fundamental causes of our belated concern. Intensified by declining economic opportunities for low-skilled, poorly educated individuals, these basic population shifts have created social and political forces that have come to influence national policy. The civil-rights revolution has served to expose many dimensions of second-class citizenship, and the "social dynamite" noted by James Conant has exploded in many a city in recent years.[2] Many of the nation's school systems have found themselves in the vortex of the pressures and counterpressures resulting from these and other societal conditions.

The degrees to which urban school systems have been able to implement major curricular and organizational reforms to meet the educational needs of large numbers of children from low-income, minority-group families vary from system to system. Even the most convinced Pollyannas among educational spokesmen would hardly contend that enough has been done, however. On the contrary, it appears that the bulk of the reforms proposed are still in the pilot or experimental phases of development. A tremendous amount of work still needs to be done.

This lag should not suggest that those programs that have been implemented are mere token expressions of concern. A growing number of educators *are* concerned about the educational problems of disadvantaged youth and are seeking to implement reforms and new programs. Fundamental reforms, however, are not common. American schools have so far failed to provide the types of curricular and organizational reforms demanded to meet the needs of large numbers of children from low-income, minority-group families. The "last chance" noted by Martin Mayer has yet to be grasped.[3] Much of what schools do and represent is so entrenched in the traditions and expectations of bygone generations that such other critics as Paul Goodman and Edgar Friedenberg call for even more drastic surgery.[4] Whatever the depth of reform called for, however, it is clear that our public schools are in the midst of a crisis that cannot be resolved by words alone. Evidence of reform is demanded by many groups, and such demands will, hopefully, help to bring about more than a token response.

A case can be made for the position that educators cannot alone be held responsible for or single-handedly overcome societal conditions that are integral parts of our culture. It is obvious, however, that this line of reasoning can be used as a rationalization by those who are not eager to enter the arena of basic educational reform. It can also be demonstrated that institutions are generally afflicted by cultural lag and are not quickly responsive to changing conditions. It should not be surprising, therefore, that urban school systems are slow to change no matter how many speeches are made and how many committees are formed. Any student of education quickly learns that one of the perennial debates among educators revolves about a "can-should" dichotomy; that is, *can* educators lead society and *should* educators lead society? The question was posed most eloquently by George Counts in his book *Dare the Schools Build a New Social Order?* [5] The answer in the Depression of the 1930s was negative. The answer is still painfully clear if one examines the leadership record of the educational community in the desegregation struggle of the 1950s and 1960s. Traditions in selection and training procedures, hiring and promotion practices, and community and individual attitudes toward the proper role of the teacher combine so as to remove the bulk of American teachers from the mainstream of political and social issues. That some teachers *are* politically and socially change-oriented and that the number may be growing are not sufficiently strong counterarguments yet. Although every generation of educators has had its handful of spokesmen calling for teachers to assume leadership roles, the rank-and-file response has been minimal. Perhaps the new militancy of some teachers will reverse the tradition of emasculated withdrawal.

It is not our intent to pursue the debate at any length, however. Our concern is focused on what a beginning teacher can expect to experience in accepting a position in an urban school system, particularly if that position is in an inner-city area. In focusing on the neophyte teacher, we shall not explore all aspects of inner-city schools. Those of direct concern to the teacher and the line administrator will be analyzed, however. Since teachers make up the bulk of the professional staff in any school system, the problems, pressures, attitudes, and myths that affect teachers are of fundamental import. If a better understanding of these problems can be achieved, perhaps a more realistic attack can be made on one of the basic weaknesses in urban school systems, that is, the avoidance of inner-city schools by what appears to be the majority of teachers.

The fact that some teachers and administrators *are* interested in teaching in schools serving disadvantaged youth does not change the basic pattern of avoidance. As educators discussing this pattern sometimes wryly remark, there is no waiting list to transfer into the inner city. Although this state of affairs may be viewed with alarm, there are reasons for its existence. It is my intent to explore these reasons and to separate, when possible, facts from misconceptions. The discussion is aimed primarily at the neophyte teacher, but it will also be of interest to people contemplating teaching careers.

This book attempts to sketch a portrait of teaching careers in urban schools. It is not an exhaustive treatment. Rather, it attempts to provide two points of departure: an analysis of selected aspects of urban schools, their teachers, their problems, and their promise; and an approach to the study of inner-city schools, that is, guidelines for further analysis by the reader. It also includes the insights of several people teaching in or administering inner-city schools. People in line positions

can bring to bear first-hand experiences that simply are
not readily available to other observers of urban schools.
It is recognized that not all teachers and administrators
are perceptive analysts of their roles and of the intricate
workings of the school systems of which they are a part.
The same appraisal can be made of any occupational
group. Some teachers and administrators *are* students of
their calling, however, and their contributions are vitally needed.

Much of the literature on the problems of urban
schools focuses, quite rightly, on the characteristics of
the disadvantaged child. Frank Riessman's work *The
Culturally Deprived Child*, for example, was one of the
first books in this category and remains the best single
introduction to the field:[6] Riessman not only deals with
some of the characteristics of disadvantaged youth but
also does so in a forcible, positive manner too frequently lacking in books on education. Another excellent introduction to urban education has been written
by G. Alexander Moore, Jr., as part of Project True at
Hunter College. His *Urban School Days* offers the insightful analysis of an anthropologist observing day-by-
day behavior in several schools.[7] Works reporting the
first-hand experiences of teachers in inner-city areas are
also beginning to appear. Dorothy McGeoch's *Learning
to Teach in Urban Schools* provides a case-history approach to the first year of teaching.[8] *The Schoolchildren* is still another example of powerful classroom
scenes offered by two inner-city teachers.[9] Whether
furthered by teachers, scholars, or administrators, the
trend begun by Riessman's volume has produced a rap-

idly growing number of books, films, and articles on the disadvantaged child. Virtually every publisher between here and the Ganges River has books on urban schools and the disadvantaged on the stands or in the works. We offer a few suggestions on further readings in the Appendix.

Although an understanding of the social-psychological characteristics of the disadvantaged child is crucial, insufficient attention has been devoted to the character- istics of teachers and school systems in inner-city areas. The importance of the teacher has not been slighted, of course; one has only to recall, for example, the well- established middle-class bias of most American teachers discussed by many writers. The bulk of the literature, however, is based on the premise that, if the teacher knows the child, he can be more effective, and the child will like school, learn more, and so on. When teachers are discussed, they are often portrayed as either highly dedicated and doing well; new to the profession and floundering; "incompetent but all you can get in the inner city"; competent to teach but *not* in the inner city; or disillusioned, bitter, and awaiting transfer. As all these types can indeed be found in any large urban school, the premise that knowing more about the life of the disadvantaged child will lead to more positive teach- ing must be challenged. We do not mean that the premise is wrong, but we have little research to ac- cept it fully in any case.

We do mean that "reaching the disadvantaged" is not going to take place in the school setting until that setting is better understood. The new teacher is basi-

cally an outsider to the social "press" of the schools and
the school system in which he teaches. By "press" we
mean the total weight of formal and informal expectations, rules and regulations, and traditions and interpersonal interactions that make up any social system. To a
high degree, these factors determine a given teacher's
success in a school system, whether the teaching assignment is in the inner or in the outer city. The "reality
shock" experienced by new teachers upon entering
the profession, described by Wagenschein,[10] may be
stronger when a teacher is assigned to the inner city, but
it also has implications for the whole profession. Although an understanding of the characteristics of the
disadvantaged child is needed and much has yet to be
learned, more attention must be paid to the forces and
pressures on teachers in schools serving such children. It
may well be that the real breakthrough in improving
inner-city schools will come when these forces and pressures are better understood and modified. It is the latter
premise that this dicussion seeks to explore.

In essence, our concern here is with *what is*. We shall
outline some of the conditions in inner-city schools,
some of the relevant attitudes of teachers in such
schools, some of the major trends in urban schools, and
some of the serious issues and problems that beset big-
city school systems. Too much of what we hear and
"know" about the inner city is based on biased
knowledge, biased by our sources and sometimes by our
own prejudices. The discussion that follows seeks to acknowledge what little we know and what we *must* know
in order truly to "reach" the disadvantaged child—and

all children in our urban schools. As in all "guide-books," the discussion is biased by the guide's interests and definitions of the situation. The subjective nature of the ideas expressed is thus admitted and deliberate, but the prospect of alternative explanations is always the reader's prerogative. We turn first to defining what is meant by the "inner city," for it is far more than a geographic location.

Notes

1. Michael Harrington, *The Other America* (Baltimore: Penguin, 1963).
2. James B. Conant, *Slums and Suburbs* (New York: McGraw-Hill, 1961).
3. Martin Mayer, "Last Chance for our Schools?" *Saturday Evening Post*, 236 (September 14, 1963), 24–6 ff.
4. Paul Goodman, *Compulsory Mis-Education* (New York: Horizon, 1964); Edgar Friedenberg, *Coming of Age in America* (New York: Random House, 1963).
5. George S. Counts, *Dare the Schools Build a New Social Order?* (New York: Day, 1932).
6. Frank Riessman, *The Culturally Deprived Child* (New York: Harper, 1962).
7. G. Alexander Moore, Jr., *Urban School Days* (New York: Hunter College, 1964).
8. Dorothy McGeoch, *et al.*, *Learning to Teach in the Urban School* (New York: Teachers College Press, 1965).
9. Mary Frances Greene and Orletta Ryan, *The Schoolchildren* (New York: Pantheon, 1965).
10. Miriam Wagenschein, "Reality Shock: A Study of Beginning Elementary School Teachers" (Master's thesis, University of Chicago, 1950).

Chapter 2

Where Is
the Inner
City?

In the growing body of literature focused on the educational problems of disadvantaged youth, the term "inner-city school" has come to be widely used. Like the phrase "culturally deprived child," however, the term is not without fault. "Core-city schools" and "slum schools" are other descriptive terms often heard. The mass media have helped to popularize these several phrases, which have also become common currency in both professional and popular journals. Teachers in particular are being asked to examine their attitudes toward working with disadvantaged youth in the inner city. The term has also become a part of the vocabulary of the inchoate war, more properly skirmish, on poverty.

Much of what is associated with the concept of the inner city is negative in nature. Poverty, vice, and decay are stressed and restressed in both scholarly and popular discussions. The posssibility of physical harm to "outsiders" who might venture into the area is implicit in these discussions. Inner-city schools are usually portrayed as dingy, poorly staffed, and crowded with apathetic children. The public letter box in our newspapers occasionally yields the fears of a teacher who is assigned to one of these schools or of one whose husband will not permit her to teach in the inner city. A stabbing in or near an inner-city school is usually reported in terms that add to the "blackboard jungle" image. Within the profession, many teachers will quite openly declare that they would never teach in or return to *that* area. College student-teachers are sometimes directed away from inner-city schools by veteran teachers who tell and retell their favorite "war stories."

There are, on the other hand, occasional newspaper or television presentations that deal with special programs in inner-city schools or that cite the work of outstanding teachers working in poor areas. Even when the intent of the story is positive, however, enough background material is usually included to perpetuate the negative connotations of life and teaching in inner-city areas. To suggest that there is another side to the inner city that needs public understanding is an understatement.

Three Definitions

Without glossing over the matrix of social problems that are concentrated in inner-city areas, much of what the general public "knows" about the inner city is based on fragmentary and biased sources. There is no doubt that there are some people who simply do not want to know more about the inner city. Some are convinced that they know all they need to know about "slum dwellers," and they are not receptive to any positive facts about inner-city life. If there is one generalization that may be suggested here, it is that far too many people overgeneralize about far too many phenomena, including the nature of inner-city life. It appears clear that many teachers, both veterans and neophytes, are prone to the same tendency. Let us examine the concept of the inner city as an overgeneralization, for there is little doubt that it is exactly that.

The term "inner city" is not usually defined, for the assumption is that its meaning is clear. It obviously refers to the section of a metropolitan area that is centrally located and that holds a concentration of the socioeconomic problems that are beginning to be given some serious attention by our society. Unfortunately, this very general definition does not fully reveal the demographic concepts on which it rests. It also does not suggest the value judgments that are implicit in much of the popular discussion of the area. In an effort to clarify the concept, this discussion deals with three subdefinitions that are both explicit and implicit in what is generally meant by the term "inner city."

The three subdefinitions with which we are concerned are geographic, demographic, and what we shall call "social-psychological" for reasons that will be clear shortly. Of these three definitions, the geographic is perhaps the most readily accepted. Clearly, the inner city must exist somewhere; therefore it has a geographic location. Recalling the concentric-circle theory of urbanization, popular in an earlier era of American sociology, we might assume that the inner city must exist somewhere near or around the downtown section of a given city, perhaps in the area of transition: that is, an area of rooming houses, multiple dwellings, and small industries and businesses, an area characterized by transience among its inhabitants. Granted that such is often the case, we cannot accept the term "inner" at face value.

Is the inner city near the downtown area? Generally it is, but there are a number of reasons why the concept is becoming more and more inaccurate. Most of our major cities, for example, have undertaken token or massive urban renewal projects. Luxury apartments (dubbed "monoxide manors" by Robert Havighurst[1]) and new industrial-park areas are often exactly where the inner city should be—or where it used to be. At the other extreme, what of the pockets of poverty that are sometimes found on the edges of a major city? What of the old rural slums, some of which have been encompassed by the suburban boom? What of our freeway systems that divide our cities and redefine both transportation and living patterns? What of all the "changing neighborhoods" that once were "good places to live" and that are miles from downtown? What of neighborhood conservation efforts found in some cities? Efforts to save and rehabilitate residential areas from decay sometimes offer striking contrasts to what one is led to believe is the housing pattern in the inner city. If one accepts the geographic definition literally, one soon is troubled by glaring examples of "inner city" features that are not where they are *supposed* to be.

Most important, what of the essential fact of sociological research that demonstrates over and over again the range in values, attitudes, aspirations, and life styles found in any congested section of a city? Certainly this fact alone seriously challenges any conception of the inner city as a homogeneous area somewhere near the core of a city. In fact, we may be reminded of the phrase of one or two generations ago, "people from the other side of the tracks." Those people were the inner-city dwellers of their day, but they were generally located away from the center of the cities in the not so distant past. In short, the geographic definition is simply too inaccurate a guide, unless it is examined in relation to certain demographic data. Although the inner city can be defined in terms of certain geographic coordinates, its exact location is probably its least important feature.

By utilizing demographic data, one's search for the inner city will yield far more accurate generalizations. Although the specifications of socioeconomic factors related to urban poverty are not definitively established, there is consensus on several points. The median family income is a key delineating factor. It has been estimated that 19 per cent of all American families live within incomes of $3,000 a year.[2] An area of a city where family incomes tend to be below the over-all average for that city would probably qualify as an "inner city" area. The proportion of renting families to home-owning families can be another criterion. The condition of the homes in the area is still another. The Census classifies homes in given tracts as sound, deteriorating, or dilapidated. The higher the percentage of homes in the latter two categories, the greater the likelihood that we are seeing an inner-city area. Other indexes that may be applied are the proportion of children under eighteen years of age living away from the family unit, the proportion of divorces and broken homes, the incidence rates of communicable diseases, and so on. Most of these facts are available from the 1960 Census, although the dated nature of the figures amply demonstrates the need for more frequent censuses in the nation. We shall discuss the use of census data more fully in a later chapter. At this point, we are not suggesting that the use of such data will locate inner city areas precisely or that every dweller in any such area is necessarily disadvantaged. On the contrary, census data simply offer median figures on certain social conditions. Such figures are merely a starting point in the analysis of living conditions in any section of the city. It is clear, however, that significant differences in subcommunities in a given city may be both detected and empirically verified with the best available census data.

When the various types of demographic information are plotted on a map, the inner city begins to take shape. Important as these data are, however, they are not sufficient to identify precisely the location of the inner city. A third, overriding factor is always present, that is, a social-psychological factor. This factor is sociological in the sense that it is commonly held by a majority of our citizens and psychological in the sense that its manifestations vary from individual to individual. We are, of course, suggesting the factor of predjudice. In essence, the inner city is where *They* live! Who *They* are varies from region to region and also from era to era in our nation's history.

In this century, for example, various immigrant groups represented the "They groups" of two or three generations ago. "Hey, you Wop" or "Polak" or "Hunky" is a cry that is heard infrequently in this era, though ethnic prejudices are still very much with us. Interestingly, "Honky," a variation of "Hunky," is again in vogue as an appellation for all whites, rather than only for some Europeans. Though the "Little Italys" and "Little Germanys" are not as pronounced as they once were, some aspects of ethnic housing patterns still remain in the core cities and in the suburban satellites. It was not too many years ago that the various ethnic groups, to some degree and each in its own turn, were the "They groups" considered undesirable or a menace.[3]

In this era, as Raymond Mack and others have written, the new urban minorities are Negroes, Puerto Ricans, and southern whites.[4] Regional differences also demand the inclusion of Indians in the Southwest and Mexican-Americans in the Southwest in general and in California and Texas in particular. These categorizations are gross, of course, and much valuable time is wasted on sophomoric debates that not *all* Negroes are disadvantaged or that there are rich Indians with oil wells. And we are all certainly aware to some degree that "the times they are a changin'." Suffice it to say that the two common elements among all the social rejects of our society are those of poverty and lack of opportunity. All the exceptions to the rule and the halting progress that is being made in terms of social justice cannot hide the more basic and uglier facts of life. As a nation, we have gone farther than most in fighting and exposing some of our basic prejudices, but we still have a long way to go. Racial, ethnic, social-class, and religious prejudices are part of the American way of life. One simply cannot be inducted into our society without being conditioned to them. They become internalized. Once we acknowledge this fact, locating the inner city becomes relatively easy: It is where, in the minds of bigoted people, the social rejects of a given city are concentrated.

The Factor of Prejudice

If this premise is accepted, we still face the problem of defining our own particular "inner cities." That is, one's own favorite prejudices come into play, and one may be selective in rejecting one group or another. The social psychology of prejudice need not concern us here, nor would it be necessary to elaborate on the fact that prejudice exists on a continuum. We must each seek to determine where we may be on the scale and in which direction we, as individuals, are heading. There are certain major points of coalescence upon which our prejudices as a nation focus, the cleavage between Negroes and whites being the most obvious. For our purposes, it remains only to state, using some archaic phrases, that each major city has certain "elements" in it that the "solid citizenry" tends to reject. Wherever these "undesirables" or "untouchables" live, whatever the geographic or demographic data, *there* is where the inner city is.

In more than one discussion with groups of teachers, it has been my experience that it is not until the They concept is broached and examined that the real meaning of discussions of disadvantaged youth begins to appear. We can discuss the geographic and demographic factors with little personal involvement (unless, perhaps, we are members of the groups being discussed), but it is not until the factor of prejudice is admitted that the discussion becomes fruitful. Teachers, after all, are a fairly representative group, and it would be naïve to assume that prejudice disappears with the issuing of a teaching license. The fact that the waiting lists to transfer out of the inner city are far longer than those of teachers who want to transfer in (if the latter lists even exist) should be enough to demonstrate the extent to which prejudice may be found among teachers. It is not being suggested that teachers are any more prejudiced than the population as a whole. On the contrary, there seems to be some correlation between levels of education and the alleviation of prejudice; teachers should therefore be a cut above average. It also does little good to argue idealistically that teachers *ought* to be able to control their prejudices, as no doubt many of them do. It will be far more profitable to discuss *what is*, rather than what ought to be. Only with a firm grasp of social reality can we project trends and then make plans for influencing these trends.

At least one writer has grappled with the implications of prejudice among teachers and has taken a very strong position. Nathaniel Hickerson states:

> Deny entry into the teaching profession to all those who are not reasonably free of race-mindedness or social or economic caste-inspired intolerance. As we insist that our teachers should be academically prepared to teach their subject matter effectively, so we must insist that these same teachers not harm the children of the economically deprived through behavior based upon hostility and arrogance bred of feelings of superiority. (If this is a difficult task, consider the result if we do not exclude the intolerant from the teaching profession. Enter any one of thousands of public schools today and see the results of the presence of race and caste-minded teachers.) [5]

We recognize that the implementation of this strong directive is unlikely in the profession, but we support its intent. There is no "holier than thou" overtone either in Hickerson's view or in our acceptance of it. Prejudice toward Negro, Puerto Rican, southern white, poor, and lower-class children exists within the profession, and the first step toward destroying it is to expose it.

Unless one acknowledges the fact of prejudice in discussing the true nature of the inner city and the reaction of teachers to it, one will be discussing only the visible portion of the iceberg. And just as the iceberg is a menace to navigation, prejudice toward the poor minority groups of the nation threaten our democracy. Being frank in discussing the "They concept" tends to involve us all in the basic social issues of our society. Without such frank discussion, we shall continue to define the inner city with geographic and demographic precision and still fail to deal with what really counts.

An anecdote may further strengthen this view. Several years ago, I was supervising a student-teacher in a junior high-school social-studies class. A school-tax election was imminent and the teacher's plan indicated that he would distribute and briefly discuss some literature on the tax, which his students were then to take home to their parents. He fully intended to move on to the main topic of discussion, that is, the Romans, the Greeks, or some other ancients that dominate the social-studies curriculum; the school-tax discussion was merely a token exercise in citizenship training. The "discussion" of the school tax began with the teacher asking a few questions. Within thirty seconds it had become the standard, sing-song type of recitation that characterizes many classrooms much of the time, a phenomenon that John Holt has described perhaps definitively.[6] In any case, I was already sinking into that malaise of many supervisors in which one begins to lose hope that even one out of five classrooms visited might exhibit more than routine and dull "discussions." Then the aura of vapidity broke rather sharply. A boy simply stated that his father had said that the new tax would be used to build schools for the "coloreds" living downtown and that both father and son were against it. The iceberg of indifference had been exposed in this all-white classroom. The ninth-grader's outspokenness catalyzed other students into speaking out. For the balance of the period the classroom was alive with debate, and the student-teacher learned what a discussion can be. His task was that of a busy moderator, and he needed to say very little. About one-third of the group exhibited anti-Negro prejudices that would easily gain them KKK membership. Another third of the class presented counterarguments that challenged both the racial and anti-poor views of their peers. The balance of the class listened carefully. The debate ended as a draw, but many core values of the young American were exposed, ranging from hatred to humanism. It was the type of discussion that reveals basic attitudes, and it is the type of discussion educators need to engage in if their analyses of the disadvantaged are to be more than professional and superficial exercises.

It is said that only after we acknowledge our problems can we begin to control them. One of the crucial problems in American education is that a number of American teachers are not eager to work with disadvantaged youth. How large is that number? Obviously, very little data exists on such a sensitive question. Suffice it to say that if the number were not considerable, there would be little need for the National Teacher Corps; for all the National Defense Education Act Institutes on Disadvantaged Youth; for all the articles and books exhorting teachers to become more involved in solving the educational problems of the disadvantaged; for all the rapidly multiplying symposia, meetings, committees, and conventions focused on the disadvantaged; and for all the compensatory programs, ranging from the Higher Education Opportunities Act to Project Head Start. These efforts are all desperately needed—not only to educate children better, but also to educate their teachers better. It is the latter who are likely to gain the most in the first round of compensatory-education efforts.

Let us clarify the major point that may be misunderstood in the previous remarks. It is not being suggested that *all* teachers are prejudiced or incompetent to work with the disadvantaged. Many teachers are probably doing the best they can under trying conditions—and some of them are excellent in inner-city situations. It is unlikely that one will ever meet a school administrator, however, who would give the latter accolade to his full staff. On the contrary, the plea of most people directing the multitudes of special programs for the disadvantaged is constant: We need more competent and dedicated teachers in the inner city. There is indeed a desperate shortage of such teachers. There are several reasons why, but we shall focus on only one: the demands of the urban school system on the teacher, especially on the neophyte teacher. We do so in the belief that the internal pressures of school-system life, on students and teachers alike, are the fundamental cause of the failure of American schools to provide better education for the disadvantaged child—and all children. All the minor modifications of curriculum and compensatory services now underway cannot succeed until the basic organization of schools is altered. Aspirins are no substitute for surgery. It will certainly be necessary to create new institutions of learning if schools are not drastically reorganized in the next decade. The new teacher needs to seriously consider this point for teaching will no longer be the safe sinecure it has often been in the past. In analyzing next some of the realities of teaching in urban schools, the need for such reform will be underscored.

Notes

1. Robert J. Havighurst, "Urban Development and the Educational System," in A. Harry Passow, ed., *Education in Depressed Areas* (New York: Teachers College Press, 1963), p. 40.
2. Leon H. Keyserling, *Progress or Poverty* (Washington: Conference on Economic Progress, 1964).
3. *Cf.* Peter Isaac Rose, *They and We: Racial and Ethnic Relations in the United States* (New York: Random House, 1964).
4. Raymond W. Mack, "Changing Ethnic Fabric of the Metropolis," in B. J. Chandler, *et al.*, ed., *Education in Urban Society* (New York: Dodd, Mead, 1962).
5. Nathaniel Hickerson, *Education for Alienation* (Englewood Cliffs, N. J.: Prentice-Hall, 1966), p. 94.
6. John Holt, *How Children Fail* (New York: Pitman, 1964).

Chapter 3

Schools Are More Alike Than Different

We have already noted that most of the opinions about the inner city exchanged in both professional and lay circles are negative in nature. As McGeoch and her colleagues note:

> Teaching in slum schools is hard work. Children who have learned to distrust adults, to expect failure in school, and to settle most problems with their fists are not easy to handle. Many schools are old and crowded; classes are often large; supplies and materials are inadequate or inappropriate. Some staff members are openly waiting for transfers or are past caring for anything but their monthly paycheck. For the conscientious and competent educator, the undiscriminating community dissatisfaction with the inadequacies of the segregated urban school can be frustrating and disheartening. Little support and less recognition is the lot of the typical teacher in such a school.[1]

Although this statement is not an exaggeration, the net result of a constant stream of such generalizations could only lead and has led to a skewed portrait of inner-city education.

The simple fact is that most schools are rather tightly controlled, whether they be in the inner city or in a rural area. Schools are organized and controlled by the adults who staff them, and this means that student behavior seldom gets out of hand, though the incidence of some types of behavior are higher in the so-called "slum school." What is really frightening is not the occasional existence of a school, where, usually because of weak administration and poor staff, people begin not to give a damn and to let some of their students run wild—and it *does* occur. What is of far greater consequence is the overwhelming *sameness* of school organization, patterns of behavior, expectations, and curriculum in school after school, urban, suburban, and rural. The dull routine of most schools gives the innovator his challenge, but it also gives the conforming teacher the certainty and quiet that make his days uneventful and "satisfying."

In regard to student behavior, I have never heard of any school where students don't fight, where toilet tissue does not get scattered about, where some "outsider" seeking his girl friend does not challenge the authority of a teacher or principal, where a locker is not broken into, where there is never any smoking in the lavatory, where a window does not get broken, where some boy does not have a knife, where some nearby candy store or

hamburger joint is not considered a "den of thieves"—
to mention only a few types of troublesome behavior
found among students, particularly those in the junior
and senior high school. The incidence of these and other
types of behavior that concern teachers is amazingly low,
even in a so-called tough school. It should never be forgotten that *one* obscenity written on a school's door is
usually interpreted as the norm for the school, when it
is only the work of one or two individuals out of
hundreds and even thousands. The news of a lunchroom
fight in a large junior high school sweeps the halls as if a
prison riot had taken place, when only two, three, or
four individuals were involved. Some teachers and the
public tend to magnify incidents of this type into a dis-
torted image of what schools are really like. Obviously,
most adults would like children to behave like "little
ladies and gentlemen" all the time. Surprisingly, most
of them do. The reason that "incidents" are given all
the attention they get is because they challenge the conformity imposed on virtually all the students in any
school, and they are exceptions to the usual pattern of
school life.

The neophyte teacher, young, inexperienced, and
often frightened of children and of the bigness of
schools, may be assigned to a large urban junior high
school and be shocked by some of the behavior and
noise exhibited by young adolescents. This same
teacher may never know that he would have experienced the same behavior in a suburban junior high
school. Outgoing behavior and noise in the halls and
lunchrooms of a junior high school reflect the char-

acteristics of children at this stage of development and also reflect the organizational pattern of the typical junior high. But because the junior high schools in the inner city are likely to have Negro or other minority-group students, this behavior is considered far more threatening and deviant. Unfortunately, some teachers refuse to accept this analysis of the situation. Some become infuriated by any attempt to look objectively at student behavior and the reasons for it, raising the usual "ivory tower" charge. Like it or not, the classrooms we have observed where students run wild and the teacher is absolutely floundering are not restricted to the inner city. They can be found in many schools and in all types of socioeconomic areas.

Again, a personal anecdote may clarify our main thesis, that is, that schools are more alike than different. I was once the "enforcer" in an urban high school. My title was really "attendance teacher," and I helped counselors by making home calls about truancy, illnesses, and other reasons for extended absences. I was also expected to visit the two local restaurant hangouts periodically and to bring back the handful of students who had "skipped" study hall or gym class. In addition, I was the official school "greeter." For example, when three leather-jacketed boys with dangling cigarettes would dare to breach the school campus and stand outside a classroom window, I was expected to encourage them to move on. And I would roam the halls occasionally and check passes and so on. I was not exactly enthusiatic about these duties, and I had more than one quaking moment during the year I worked at this task.

What happened during that year is interesting: I was never struck by a student or even seriously challenged. The point is that students, even the truant or drop-out hanging around the campus, know that most high schools have "an enforcer." My appearance alone in my role as the enforcer was enough to have students say "Here he comes. Let's move on." And the handful of "tight" confrontations never really hit the boiling point. Not that I was particularly adept at the job or that some guy couldn't have squared off and scared the life out of me—but it just didn't happen. The point of this tale is not my performance, however. This high school was an all-white high school in an all-white, "highly desirable" section of the city—the type of school that many teachers and the lay public view as ideal. This school had every behavior problem found in an inner-city school. It was not as crowded and its staff was essentially an experienced one, so the incidence of problems was lower, but the problems were there, as they are in every school. There were apathetic students, eager students, and maladjusted students in almost every classroom. If one is convinced, however, that inner-city schools are awful and dangerous, neither this anecdote nor a hundred like it will sway the tide of prejudice against and fear of the inner-city school.

Some Premises

There are, therefore, alternate ways of viewing the inner-city school. We will stress a more positive approach, which has at least five major premises.

First and foremost, most schools are far more alike than they are different—*no matter what area they serve*. Many people who are "shocked" by the behavior they see in an inner-city school would be just as shocked by the same behavior in any school. They are shocked simply because they have little concept of how schools are organized, how some students behave, how some teachers behave, and so on.

Our emphasis is on the word *some*. We are suggesting that there are variations on the themes of teaching and learning in all schools, and very few schools—inner-city or outer city—are outstandingly different. The neophyte teacher will experience many of the same rewards and frustrations of teaching in any school.

Second, children exhibit a wide range of behavior in all schools. Any person who assumes that all children in an inner-city school can't or don't want to learn knows very little about children and learning. There are children in *all* schools who are not interested in learning or who are difficult to reach. One may ask if the incidence or percentage of certain types of behavior is higher in one type of school or another, and there is value in this question. No doubt there is a greater concentration of teaching and learning problems in some inner-city schools than in others. What is done about these problems is the big question, however. Some teachers and administrators strive hard to alleviate these problems in a dozen ways. At the other extreme, some teachers would rather quit than enter an inner-city school. They simply *know* that it is not the place for them—and they are probably right! If they are so set in their ways, one

might well question just how good they are as teachers
in *any* setting. If a teacher is unaware of his students'
backgrounds and is unwilling to examine variations in
his methods and materials, regardless of where he
teaches, he is probably a rotten teacher—which is not a
polite description but is most appropriate.

Third, some teachers and administrators are better
than others in inner-city schools. Some schools are
"happy ships," and others are akin to "sinking ships."
Any experienced teacher knows of inner-city schools
whose staffs do very good jobs. In others, however, there
is much to be desired. This same comment can be made
of any school, of any teaching staff, and of any school
system. Just because a school is in the inner city, an
unhappy or incompetent staff is not a necessary corollary. On the contrary, great variations in morale exist
from building to building in any major school system.

Fourth, although ethnic, racial, religious, regional,
and other subcultural variations do exist in our society,
many values and aspirations are shared by all Americans. Anyone who assumes that inner-city children and
parents hate school and teachers and will not cooperate
or are not willing to learn is a poorly informed person.
People are not *that* different anywhere. The problem of
motivating youth to learn in our society is common to
schools in any location. If one teaches in an area of the
city where a higher percentage of children come from
broken homes or live in economic conditions that do
not give them a very rich background for schooling, he
may find it harder to reach his students. Not all inner-
city children come from such backgrounds, however.

Even if they did, the choice is clear: Either teachers do
things differently in order to reach them more effectively, or the schools help to perpetuate inequities in
our society. Educators must make a choice: Are they
going to help solve these problems or not?

Last, but not least, if we are willing to examine our-
selves, that is, our values, prejudices, motivations, and
capabilities, we can go a long way toward reaching any
students we teach. We tend to assume that a teacher in
a middle-class area, where a higher percentage of children are being pushed at home to do well in school, is a
good teacher. The fallacy of such reasoning requires little discussion. Unfortunately, this point is not debated
openly. It is simply accepted as part of the traditional
wisdom of education, both within and outside the profession. Given these statements of position, let us examine in more detail the thesis that schools are more alike
than they are different. We shall focus on four interrelated concepts: schools as social systems, the expectations of the system, the individual's adaptation to the
system, and the first year as a teacher.

Schools as Social Systems

The sociology of education provides us with ample
documentation that schools, like all other institutions,
can be profitably analyzed as types of social systems.
The concept of system is quite simple. It rests on the
premise that any complex organization may be dissected
so that its component parts are identified and their interrelationships and contributions to the system re-

vealed. We shall analyze only a few selected aspects of schools. For example, schools are subdivisions of a bureaucratic structure that encompasses state laws, local boards of education, the rules and regulations of such systems, and the traditional forms of organization and teaching associated with each curriculum area. Every major school system has a "downtown" office. There the superintendent, his staff, supervisors, and a host of other functionaries handle the administration of the school system. The neophyte teacher must pass through the grid of hiring procedures and other routines associated with finding a position. It is at this point that he usually has his first and sometimes only contact with the central office.

As many newcomers to the system learn, getting into the system and learning one's role in it are like the old army game; that is, one learns to do things "by the numbers." It is difficult to discuss schools as social systems without overgeneralizing. For example, most school systems have personnel departments that are very concerned about recruiting new teachers, making them feel that they are important to the system and that grand careers await them in the system. Sometimes even the most well-meaning personnel directors cannot achieve their goals, however, simply because they must hire anywhere from one to three or four thousand teachers every year. Because they are dealing with very large numbers and because it is almost in the nature of bureaucracy that depersonalization takes place, many a new teacher who feels welcome during a personal interview is given the brush-off by clerks who "handle" the teacher in later stages of the game. For example, it is possible in a large system for a teacher to be hired by "downtown" only to find when he reports to his building that the principal was unaware that he was coming. The principal will probably handle this incident in a smooth manner, but the impact on the neophyte is "Don't they know what they are doing?" At the other extreme, some smaller school systems in the nation make it a practice to give the "red carpet" treatment to the prospective teacher. They not only interview him, but they also introduce him to all the key people at his school. He will be shown the very room and supplies he will be using, and all of the benefits of the system will be explained in a way that makes the neophyte feel very much at home. Large city school systems would probably like to follow the same procedure, but the numbers of applicants and the numbers of people who handle the applicants are so large that there can be a tremendous difference in the experiences of any two teachers applying to the same urban school system.

The impact of "downtown" is much wider than the initial contact might suggest. Every major school system has within it a chain of command that is usually clear cut and rigid. But even this eternal verity is being altered as teachers' organizations gain power through collective bargaining. To the neophyte teacher, however, the overwhelming press of expectations and directives from "downtown" are a social fact. The bureaucratic structure of any school system represents the power of that system, and power is the social cement that maintains all institutions. The beginning teacher is very near the bottom of the bureaucratic totem pole. His power is limited, for power in a social system is akin to interest in a bank. The newcomer must be in the system some time before his knowledge of its workings is sufficiently insightful so that he can learn in which directions his personal power is effective and how he can multiply it.

The chain of command in any major school system is a fact that the neophyte teacher quickly learns to respect; otherwise, he learns the price of challenging it. In the typical school, the power of both traditional and codified school law is focused in the person of the principal. It had been said, *before* collective bargaining, that the principal of a school is similar in many ways to the captain of a ship. All major decisions pass through his hands, and it is within his power to intercede in virtually all operations in the school. We recognize that all principals do not utilize their power in the same way. Research has begun to establish the concept of administrative styles. Principals can be placed in categories based on analysis of their typical courses of action as they work with their superiors, their faculties, and the children in their schools. The station of the principal, however, is a fact that most neophyte teachers are aware of. Their own experiences as children, usually reinforced by their practice-teaching experiences, generally make it clear that the principal is someone with power, authority, and prestige. In short, he is the boss, and most teachers are very cognizant of their relationship to the boss.

Discovering the chain of command is much more intricate than simply identifying the principal as a key figure. The neophyte teacher will gradually learn that in every school some teachers enjoy far more prestige and power than do others. *Sometimes*, and this qualification must be stressed, prestige and power are based on the abilities of the teacher to get children to learn. Teaching ability is only *one* criterion of prestige and power in the school system. In many elementary schools, for example, teachers who started teaching the eighth grade as young women and now, some twenty-five years later, still handle the eighth grade are deferred to by all; in many ways they are viewed as the principals' right hands. Seasoned teachers sometimes operate as assistant principals without portfolio; experience and longevity establish their position in the school. These teachers often get the "best room" and "best supplies" year after year. Still other teachers who perform special functions in the school, for example, handle used book sales, arrange graduation exercises, control the school newspaper, and so on, also enjoy reputations and prestige that the newcomer may envy. Certainly they represent areas of interest that the new teacher cannot enter without some experience and without some careful footwork designed to avoid moving in on the experienced teacher's territory.

Teachers who simply know how to control students, at any level of education, are sometimes deemed of utmost importance to the operation of the school. They may be shop teachers, homeroom teachers, or counselors; whoever they are, they have the reputation of being "enforcers." Every teacher and child in the building knows that these people can and do maintain order. As the maintenance of order is one of the highest ideals of most schools, the value of such teachers is greatly enhanced. Some new teachers who are having difficulties in classroom management may envy these Gestapo prototypes. Other newcomers who are committed to the abolition of corporal punishment will be repelled by what they see and hear. Both reactions will be accepted by the system for they reflect one of the continual internal battles among teachers.

The neophyte also quickly learns that there is a pecking order among teachers based on the subjects they teach, particularly among secondary-school teachers. Science and mathematics teachers are considered brighter than English and social-studies teachers. Whether this belief is valid or not is of no consequence; it is simply one of the society-wide beliefs that is reflected in any large high school. At the other extreme, shop and vocational classes are sometimes used as dumping grounds for students who find it difficult to adjust to academic subjects or behavior standards. Because they work with academic rejects, it follows that shop teachers are a lesser breed than their academic colleagues. College-preparatory teachers are "better" than business-education teachers; teachers who work with older children are "more mature" than those who work with younger children; teachers who teach in the "best schools" are several levels above those who teach in disadvantaged areas; and so on.[2]

We must stress that these comments are not being offered as what ought to be. These attitudes are commonly held, however, and they are part of the social atmosphere of schools. We expect the perceptive teacher to see through the flimsiness of the pecking orders established in most schools. Many will not, however; they will accept the traditional wisdom and will behave accordingly. Perception is likely to develop faster if the newcomer has some concept of what to expect. Though the individual teacher may see through the weak standards of who "counts" and who "doesn't count," the fact remains that faculties as a whole will act on the basis of the informally derived pecking order.

The web of role interrelationships and patterns of deference and rejection that exist within any large school are all parts of the concept of the school as a social system. The administrative staff of the school, the teaching staff, the secretaries, the custodial staff, and the student body may each be analyzed as components of the broader system. The neophyte teacher lacks the experience that would help him to identify readily the roles played by each of these major components, as well as the more subtle subroles within each category. He may not learn for many months that perhaps his greatest ally is neither the "buddy" teacher assigned to him by the principal to help in his first months of teaching, nor his department head, nor any of the other people in the chain of command. On the contrary, the janitor or secretary may be the most helpful. The elementary-school teacher, for example, will probably learn that in female-dominated elementary schools, male janitors frequently play roles that extend far beyond the tending of fires and the spreading of wax. In some elementary schools, where the only male figure is the janitor, his power and

prestige are attributed directly to the factor of sex alone.
In any school, however, the teacher who feels superior
to the janitor and acts accordingly may quickly learn
that, when a child vomits in his room, the janitor may
be very difficult to locate and will take a great deal of
time in coming to clean up the mess. To put it another
way, there may even be occasions when the janitor gives
the teachers orders. It is not uncommon for some well-
established janitors to point out to the neophyte teacher
that too much paper is left on the classroom floor after
school and that he is not about to work harder in that
room when most other teachers have their children
clean up the rooms. Another janitor may complain to a
teacher who engages in group work that he does not approve of having to return the chairs to their traditional
spots on the floor.

The school secretary is another key figure in the informal chain of command who can make the difference
between a happy and an unpleasant day at school. Because virtually all school business passes over the secretary's desk, the teacher who is "in" with her will often
get prior notice of some problem, a friendly word of
advice about a coming order, or some gossip that the
teacher should know. In some schools the secretaries
feel superior to the teachers and act accordingly. I recall
one high school where the chief secretary took responsibility for all paper supplies. The faculty estimated that
she had enough paper, pencils, and related supplies to
keep the school running for fifty years. She was very
stingy in allocating those supplies; teachers would receive two pencils, a box of clips, and a blank pad for

small messages once every year. Teachers simply were not successful in getting additional supplies from that secretary unless they had her on their side.

We do not intend to suggest that janitors and secretaries control schools. On the contrary, most janitors and secretaries "know their places," just as most teachers and students "know their places." Nor are we suggesting that either principals, janitors, or secretaries conspire to make work difficult for the teacher. Most teachers will have very happy experiences with all these people and will find them both friendly and supportive. Our point is to stress that the formal chain of command, which one learns as a student in school and then during his training for teaching, does not always operate the way organization charts indicate. Either the beginning teacher learns to recognize the informal powers that are in his building, or his effectiveness is lessened. Effectiveness has very little to do with how competent or dedicated he may be in working with children because a good deal of his anxieties and satisfactions are *not* related to the work of his classes.

Still another aspect of the school as a social system is the unbalanced ratio of women to men in education. Approximately two-thirds of all American teachers are female. In the elementary schools, women outnumber men about nine to one. At the secondary level, the ratio is approximately fifty-fifty, with men sometimes outnumbering women in large high schools. We have come a long way since the feminist movement at the turn of the century, but to some degree women still remain second-class citizens. Although the logic may not be perfect, a profession made up largely of second-class citizens can hardly have the stature of a profession like medicine, which is made up almost exclusively of men. Our concern, however, is not with the usual polemics associated with the virtue and/or value of having more men in the profession. We certainly are not suggesting that men are necessarily better teachers than women. We *are* suggesting two factors. First, it is already well established that the feminization of schools has a strong impact on the development of young children. Sexton and others have suggested, for example, that children coming from matriarchal backgrounds have little chance of identifying with males in female-dominated elementary schools.[3]

We are even more concerned with a second major implication, that is, that any male accepting a teaching position must recognize the probability of working within a profession that is largely dominated by females. Although this domination is not as pervasive at the secondary level, there is little reason to dispute the fact that few males enter elementary teaching, not only because of the social pressures against men working with younger children, but also because males perforce would be greatly outnumbered by females on the staffs of elementary schools. We have already noted how the janitor in the elementary school may play a role beyond his designated position simply because he may be the only male in a school. We might suggest that a male who wishes to gain stature *should* enter elementary teaching, as he will have little competition from other males, and the odds of his gaining prestige and promotion are probably greater than at the secondary level. People concerned with attracting more males to the profession sometimes urge a differential pay scale, a reversion to an earlier day in the profession, when male teachers were paid more. Although a differential pay scale based on sex would create inequities in terms of other criteria, at least the proposal faces up to the problems created by a skewed sexual ratio. Whatever the remedy, the feminization of American education is one of the facts of life, and no attempt to outline the school as a social system can ignore it. Perhaps the recent legislation designed to equalize male-female employment patterns will have an impact on the problem.

The several aspects of the school as a social system outlined so far exist in every school. Whether a school be serving a suburban middle-class area or an inner-city working-class area, the social facts of life are essentially the same. The teachers, administrators, students, custodial staff, and parents in the immediate community are all parts of an intricate web of relationships and functions. The beginning teacher who expects to enter the system and do his job without becoming "involved" with all the other aspects of the system is simply "out of it." He just does not understand what he is getting into. The day-to-day life of the teacher in any school demands that he learn the expectations of all the components of the social system of which he is a part. His behavior as a teacher is evaluated by his colleagues, by his supervisors, sometimes by parents, and literally every second by the children with whom he works. He in turn has expectations of what the other components of the system mean to him. If he is to survive in the system, the teacher must somehow balance his expectations with those of the rest of the system.

It is quite possible that the potentially effective teacher may become so involved in the web of interrelationships in his school that his powers to innovate within the system are limited. As difficult as it is for us as individuals to accept, particularly in a democracy, the system almost always wins. If one enters a school system in which he is merely a teacher among 5,000 other teachers, it becomes rather obvious that his impact on the rest of those teachers is severly limited. Here we immediately run into a variety of arguments that have the implicit premise that "this is not the way it ought to be." We are not suggesting that this is the way it "ought to be," but it is far more realistic to establish at the outset that the neophyte teacher is a minor part of any major school system. It occasionally happens that the new teacher does acquire prestige and leadership potential in a given building or even in a given school system. It does not happen by accident, however. In fact, the odds are against its happening. We shall return to these factors for it is important to note that there are possibilities for innovation when both honesty and realism dictate that the vast majority of beginning teachers will not rock the routine operation of the schools. The neophyte teacher must learn the ways of the school system before he can find ways to work within that system and sometimes upon that system. Dewy-eyed idealism (one might write "Dewey"-eyed idealism) on the part of the beginning teacher is not necessarily the best weapon with which to enter a battle. Some of the young people who are eager to work in urban schools too often enter the fray with little more than their idealism. It is no wonder that some of them cannot survive and become effective.

The school is not quite a "total institution," as defined by Erving Goffman; that is, an institution with strong encompassing tendencies that condition all activities within it.[4] It is developing in this direction, however. Prisons, tuberculosis sanitoriums, monasteries, army camps, and similar institutions are examples of closed systems, and schools share some of their characteristics: Their structure is centralized and bureaucratic, their activities are conducted in such a way that all the people within them do the same things together, and their activities are prearranged and scheduled hour by hour and day by day. There also exists a strong distinction between inmates and staff in Goffman's analysis and between students and teachers in our application of his work. Goffman's analysis of constraints, sanctions, and privileges in total institutions has a direct applicability to the school. The simple acts of eating, choosing dress, talking to a peer, and attending to bodily needs become problematic, that is, they can only be performed within tolerances set by the institution. The individual's range of freedom is severely limited. Although education is ideally a process leading to self-development and self-expression, the rigid structure of schools places serious restrictions on the individual. There are differences be-

tween schools and completely closed institutions, but
the parallels are more striking. It is also striking how few
school people recognize this phenomenon.

It is implicit in this description that the structure of
the school impinges on both the student and the
teacher. Mortimer Kreuter has commented on the in-
fantile status to which many teachers are reduced once
they enter large school systems. Two of his comments
are especially germane to our discussion. He writes:

> Teachers are graded and inspected very much like chil-
> dren. Their private formulations for teaching their classes
> —their plan-books—are made the subject of weekly in-
> spections. They are also graded on loyalty, dress, deport-
> ment, punctuality and attendance, and evidences of
> growth . . . as are the children. What is worse, the chil-
> dren recognize that their teachers are being checked and
> graded. One has only to notice how they close ranks to
> protect a teacher when the principal makes his rounds.

Noting that some teachers bring their lunches in brown
paper bags and the lack of opportunity for adult inter-
change in the tightly packed school day, he also writes:

> From the standpoint of modern personnel practices,
> teachers work under sweatshop conditions. They literally
> have no time to go to the toilet, and when they must,
> they are obliged to summon a next door teacher to keep
> an eye on the classroom. They must punch time clocks
> twice daily and file affidavits when ill. A principal I
> know became a hero to his staff when he broke the time
> clock in his school, knowing full well that the Mainte-
> nance Bureau would never get around to fixing it.

> Such instances of check and counter-check are not de-
> scribed to draw out the horrors of bureaucracy. These
> are too well known. Rather, I want to show that they
> have a bearing on the content and methodology of teach-

ing in the city schools. I am suggesting that in all our efforts to bring innovation and creativity into the teaching profession, we must first come to grips with the teacher's infantilization at the hands of the system. Unless we get at the teacher's brown-paper-bag mentality, we shall never begin to deal with his professional problems.[5]

Although not all systems are as restrictive as the one Kreuter describes, the basic tenor of his remarks rings true. Only a teacher who anticipates the subtle aspects of the infantilizing process described by Kreuter has a chance of freeing himself from it. Unfortunately, not many teacher educators are candid enough to apprise college students of what realistically to expect. Even student teaching is likely to be a type of incubation that keeps the neophyte ignorant of the full range of pressures, responsibilities, and *opportunities* teaching presents.

Willard Waller put it best when he described the separate culture of the school. His seminal discussion of the customs, traditions, taboos, and ceremonies associated with the school is a landmark in the sociological analysis of schools. In the oft cited paragraph quoted here, Waller describes the essence of this separate culture:

> There are, in the school, complex rituals of personal relationships, a set of folkways, mores, and irrational sanctions, a moral code based upon them. There are games, which are sublimated wars, teams, and an elaborate set of ceremonies concerning them. There are traditions, and traditionalists waging their world-old battle against innovators. There are laws, and there is the problem of enforcing them. There is *Sittlichkeit*. There are specialized

societies with a rigid structure and a limited membership. There are no reproductive groups, but there are customs regulating the relations of the sexes. All these things make up a world that is different from the world of adults. It is this separate culture of the young, having its locus in the school, which we propose to study. . . .[6]

It is into this world of the young that the teacher enters; and from the moment of entrance the system designed to educate the young also takes hold of the adults charged with this responsibility. Every rule and regulation, every procedure and tradition, and every assignment and evaluation designed to educate the child has a corollary impact on the teachers and administrators enforcing the rules, acting out the traditions, and encouraging the learning. How to meet the expectations of the system and yet remain an individual, how to be creative and professional when all about are pressures to "do the job" are dilemmas each teacher must face. Only a small percentage find positive resolutions.

The Press of Expectations

Whatever school system a teacher joins, the demands placed on him to behave in ways appropriate to the role of teacher are overwhelming. How the teacher dresses, how he speaks, how he relates to his peers, how he talks about the children with whom he works, and a myriad of other factors are part of the expectations related to the role he now fulfills. Havighurst and Neugarten describe six major roles that all teachers play: mediator of learning, surrogate of middle-class authority, disciplinarian, parent substitute, judge, and confidant.[7] Many other subroles can be added. Any teacher quickly learns that in the school, as in all bureaucracies, forms and paper work are almost ends in themselves. Therefore a seventh and major role might be that of bookkeeper. Our point is not to analyze in any detail how teachers perform these various roles: The fact remains that they must perform *all* of them. Most neophyte teachers enter their new positions with a modicum of skill related to the role of "mediator of learning," that is, the ability to organize materials and learning experiences for children. To some neophyte teachers, teaching means merely putting page numbers on the board and giving tests; to others it is the full panorama of activities sometimes called "the art of teaching."

What the neophyte is not prepared for is the fact that he must play all the other roles concurrently and must even learn them all virtually in one day. Many teachers would argue that they never wanted to be disciplinarians. Such arguments are generally meaningless for people usually fail to establish what is meant by the word "disciplinarian." According to Havighurst and Neugarten, to be a disciplinarian simply means to know how to manage groups of children. Obviously, some teachers achieve this end by acting like storm troopers. At the other extreme, we also know of the "little old lady" teacher, whom we have all met somewhere in our career, who never raises her voice or sends a student from the room and yet has remarkable "discipline." As we are not concerned with the details of teaching, but rather with the adjustment of the neophyte into the system of teaching, we need only stress that acquiring the proper behavior associated with the several subroles noted before is a formidable task for any neophyte. It is sometimes said that the first year of teaching is the most difficult, and this statement again is true whether one is speaking of a school in a disadvantaged area or in one that is in suburbia or, more vividly, "white land."

The way in which the individual learns his roles is of course influenced by variations in his training, his personality makeup, and the support or lack of support he receives from his peers. It is clear, however, that schools are among the most rigid of our social institutions. The choices presented to teachers as to how to behave in front of the class or on the public forum are quite limited. That the nature of behavioral demands is *beginning* to change does not ease the pressure of traditions to any great degree. What teachers will be like twenty years from now is a matter both for speculation and extrapolation. At this juncture, however, teachers must still behave basically as authoritarians, as most school systems are predicated on a system of hierarchy and authority.

John Holt, Paul Goodman, and others are among the small group of writers who are beginning to challenge seriously the relevance of what goes on in most classrooms and in most school systems. As they exist today, most schools are very much like penal institutions. If we were to remove the roof from most schools and compare them to roofless prisons, one would notice some differences; for example, the cells are smaller in prison. The over-all impression, however, would be one of the similarity between prisoners and students and wardens and teachers. Not that the goals of prisons and schools are similar, for they obviously are not. But two rather glaring similarities do exist. Schools, like prisons, handle masses of people whose every moment within the institution is controlled. Routines become important, if not ends in themselves. From the time the child enters the building to the time he leaves, he is very rarely unsupervised and unobserved by teachers. He moves when they ask him to move or permit him to move. In some schools, even his movements through the hall resemble the prison shuffle of early James Cagney films. He engages in tasks that are chosen solely by his teachers. An even more striking similarity is that both prisons and schools remove their clients from the broader society for given lengths of time. Employment patterns in our society are such that there is little room and little need for young people until after they have completed schooling, and that time might be long past high-school graduation in a growing number of cases.

If the typical school is a bureaucratic, standardized, penal-like institution, the effects upon the children in it must be of serious concern. We need to be equally concerned about the effects of such an institution on the staff operating it. To put it another way, institutions determine the means by which we achieve goals. Even teachers who seek to be creative in their attempts to teach children find themselves restricted by patterns of organization, time limitations, lack of adequate teaching materials, ritualized behavior, and the overwhelming number of children to be served. We do not intend to stress the gloomy aspects of school, for despite the factors noted, many teachers and many students do find satisfactions within the structure. A teacher in an urban classroom, who must work with four or five groups of children each day—each group comprising thirty-five to forty students and representing the full range of individual differences found in any school group of that size, can often be quite effective. Despite the restrictions of time and supplies, such teachers are able to motivate groups to look forward to being with them and to engaging in the types of activities they organize.

Exceptions to the rule do not in any manner change the basic pattern of school organization and teaching that exist, however. That some teachers and some students do well in the system is not necessarily a strong argument for the system. The crucial fact is that students, teachers, and administrators in the bulk of American schools are so caught in well-established patterns of organization and behavior that opportunities to restructure the system in any fundamental way are seriously hampered. All too often, curricular reform does not mean much more than changing one textbook for another. There are some signs that more serious reforms are being tested, thanks mainly to a large number of Federally sponsored programs over the last decade. But schools today still very much resemble schools of ten years ago, twenty-five years ago, and perhaps even fifty years ago. They have become larger, some construction techniques have been altered, there are a few rooms that are different because certain new curricular areas have been adopted, the lighting is better, and some schools are beginning to look more airy and open in contrast to the prison-like models that predominate.

What goes on in the physical confines of the school is the crucial question. It is obvious that experiments with many new approaches to teaching are being carried out. After all, professional educators have been beating their heads and breasts for generations in attempts to introduce more effective organizational patterns, materials, and approaches to teaching. A case can be made that slow but steady progress is being made in a number of curricular areas; but the progress is very, very slow. Schools are more alike than they are different not only in terms of urban-suburban comparisons, but in terms of comparisons with an earlier time. The sing-song recitation of an elementary school of three or four decades ago is repeated day in and day out in schools today. The overwhelming, stultifying, all-mighty power of a single textbook for a single subject is still the rule. Despite all the attacks on the single textbook approach, despite all the efforts of many innovative and creative teachers who have sought to break the textbook barrier, the rule still applies. The majority of teachers in every school in the nation still teach from *the* book. Most of these teachers still stand in front of a class of thirty-five to forty children. These teachers are involved basically in mass education, and all the protestations that individual differences must be met have had little impact on them.

Despite all the social, remedial, and ameliorative services that large school systems seek to provide for students not succeeding in the average classroom, the overwhelming majority of children are still in school systems that are very much like assembly lines in a factory.[8] Each child moves down the line in a group, and each teacher is responsible to put this or that into the child within the time limits that the teacher has with him. In most classrooms, children engage in tasks that they did not plan, that they do not comprehend, and that are essentially only busy work for all concerned. And as the child progresses through the system, the probability that he will develop apathetic behavior is enormous. One has only to walk the halls of any major school in any large school system and glance in the doors to observe this fact. I have had occasion to do so hundreds of times. In a given junior or senior high school, for example, one can walk by thirty or forty rooms and observe in perhaps only three or four of those rooms that some type of spirited activity is underway. Perhaps a teacher is indeed having a discussion rather than a recitation; perhaps in some arts or vocational rooms students are engaged in work in which they take pride; perhaps a music class evinces a truly cooperative spirit among a group of singers. But in the other rooms, one will simply observe students copying work off the board, sitting listlessly and listening to a teacher, glancing out the window, and giving 101 other signs of boredom and anomie. Many of the teachers give the same signs, simply going through the motions of beginning and ending classes but not really caring about what they accomplish. This picture is the reflection of social reality as we have observed it in fifteen years of experience in the public schools. In short, the neophyte teacher is not entering a profession that is as exciting as some educational writers suggest. He is entering a system of education that is overburdened and smothered in traditional approaches yet one that is seeking to accomplish a heroic task under these conditions. Although it has problems, the system is complex enough to offer much potential to the newcomer. Let us turn next to a discussion of the staff in a given school. Our line of argument can be exemplified most clearly by analyzing some of the characteristics of the teaching staff in any large school.

Adapting to the System

We are not concerned here with an examination of the social characteristics of teachers. This subject is treated in greater depth in a number of works, and an overwhelming amount of evidence suggests that teachers in the 1960s are being drawn more and more from heterogeneous sources. That is, the image of the teacher as someone coming from the middle class is no longer viable; nor was the matter ever that simple. In many major cities, a growing number of teachers are coming from working-class homes, and many of these teachers are entering the middle class via the teaching profession. Whatever their origins, however, the majority of teachers reflect the values and behavior representative of the middle class. We are concerned here not so much with class origins as with the impact of teacher training upon the prospective teacher and with the range of abilities teachers exhibit once they are in a line position in the schools.

The cornerstone of teacher training is an internship
or a student-teaching experience. There are many variations in training patterns across the nation, but the
value of direct experience with students under the supervision of an experienced teacher is one aspect of
teacher training upon which even its severest critics
agree. Yet it is the concentration on student teaching
that largely ensures that new teachers entering the profession will essentially conform to the system. Their
training, grades, and job opportunities all hinge on their
ability to adjust to the demands of the system. Even
though student teachers may be enjoined by their in-
structors to seek ways to ameliorate the system, the facts
of life are plain: It is their responsibility to adjust to the
system and not the reverse. Our point is not to examine
alternative ways of preparing teachers, for we are mainly
concerned with conditions already existent in the
schools. Our major point is that by the time he is graduated from his teacher-training institution, the neophyte
teacher has already been conditioned and is predisposed
to adjust to the schools as they are.

Once the neophyte enters the school system, he
quickly learns that he is near the bottom of the pecking
order. The types of classes assigned to him sometimes
reflect this fact, as does the school to which he is assigned; it is often a "hard school," as he does not
have the seniority necessary to expedite a transfer to a
"good school." Let us assume, however, that we are
dealing here with a neophyte who is not completely
conditioned to the system and is interested in working
in it to the best of his ability by seeking ways to improve

teaching in urban schools. Very likely, one of the first things a neophyte will learn is that, unless he is in a rare school, he will find little support for innovation or creative teaching among the rest of the faculty. If he is on a faculty composed of thirty-five to forty other teachers, it will not take him long to categorize the teaching staff into several distinct groups. He will quickly identify the old-timers. They are a group of teachers who have been in the system and in the building for perhaps fifteen or twenty years. They have learned to survive. Most of them have well-ordered, well-disciplined, well-managed classrooms in which there are activities every day that keep the children busy and, to all appearances, "happy in their work." There probably will be one or two of these old-timers who, even though they still go through the ritualized motions of teaching day in and day out, have in effect retired on the job. That is, the school is a place they go to at eight and leave at three, and there are certain things they do in between. What they do, is never debated, analyzed, or altered; they are in a rut.

Perhaps we can best continue our characterization of the teachers in a building by modifying and applying Robert Merton's typology of individual adaptation to a social system.[9] Although not concerned with teachers or schools per se, Merton suggests that there are five patterns of adaptation to any social system: conformity, innovation, ritualism, retreatism, and rebellion. It is difficult to establish whether or not the teacher who has retired on the job is exhibiting a pattern of retreatism or of conformity. Retiring on the job is a common phenomenon in many institutions; it is so common that it may well be analyzed as an aspect of conformity within the system. Be that as it may, let us examine each of the patterns of adaptation in some detail, beginning with the concept of conformity.

The neophyte will observe that the majority of teachers have conformed to the expectations of the system. Not that they work like automatons or that they all do things exactly the same way. They also gripe and occasionally show some inspiration. But the people in the system basically accept both its goals and the means to reach them within that system. In other words, teachers who have conformed to the school system generally agree with the goals of public education, the most common types of school organization, the types of teaching methodologies utilized, the ways of handling children urged by the system, and so on. Their agreement does not mean that they are necessarily effective in helping to make the system run. It also does not mean that conformity precludes criticism of the system. Most systems also provide various committees and supervisory boards that seek to improve the system to some degree. Conformity, in other words, does not mean complete acceptance of the system, but it does mean a strong tendency in that direction.

The neophyte will also observe some teachers who can be classified as innovators. They are a very small group of teachers, perhaps no more than one or two in a faculty of fifty. The innovators accept the goals of the system but seriously question the means for achieving those goals. They soon gain a reputation among their peers for seeking better ways of working with students, for creating new materials, and for improving the system or the school. They always seem to be in the forefront of change, working on some project and not afraid to be identified publicly as attempting to reach students in different ways. They are very frequently the first in the building to test out a new curriculum or a new pattern of organization.

Still another group may be described as ritualists. They are teachers who no longer care about the goals of public education but who identify themselves so closely with the means that they go through the motions of teaching, caring little about the origins or effectiveness of their procedures. They are the teachers who have reduced the art of teaching to a job. They enforce the rules without ever analyzing why the rules are there. They use the books and supplies given them without considering alternate ways of using these materials. They react to the chain of command, to the messages, to the demands upon them as parts of the job one must tolerate, and they do as much or as little as they need to do to keep in good graces with the administration. Some of these people may do an effective job simply because they have ritualized their behavior to such an extent that they may well be the best organized teachers in the school, and some students, teachers, and administrators respond to this type of organization positively. At the same time, these teachers are an embarrassment to their colleagues.

Still another group might be called the retreatists. The retreatist not only is no longer concerned with the goals of the system; he really has no concern with the means toward achieving those goals either. In essence, he might be the teacher who, after five, ten, or twenty years in the system, has learned through daily painful experience that he was never really cut out to be a teacher. Yet his pattern of life is set, and he sees no way out of his occupation. He goes through the motions of the job, but he could not care less about any aspects of it beyond his own personal comforts and his pay check. Some of these teachers have in effect retired on the job; some of them are extremely sour and bitter about children and any efforts to improve the operation of schools. They are "losers" in the system, and they will conform only so that they will not be fired. As the traditions of teaching have clearly established that incompetence is not cause for dismissal, the retreatist will probably be transferred from school to school. He will probably be able to ride it out until pension time arrives, and he may even earn the equivalent of a gold watch.

The last type of adaptation suggested by Merton is that of rebellion. The rebel wants to change the goals of the system as well as the means to achieve the goals. It is safe to say that the number of rebels in any school system is extremely small, if not nonexistent. In order to arrive at this conclusion, we must distinguish between the innovator and the rebel. The innovator accepts the goals of the system and is prepared to improve the system by challenging the means. The rebel, on the other hand, challenges both the goals and the means of the system. The probability of a rebel completing teacher training and being hired by the system is very slim. He will simply be weeded out in both the training and the hiring procedures common to educational institutions. In fact, the rebel is probably not even attracted to teaching simply because of the traditional overtones of the profession. It may be suggested that some of the people in the civil-rights movement and others who are very critical of educational practices are the types of people who would be classified as rebels if they were *within* the system. As they influence the schools from outside the system, they are not truly rebels in the typology suggested here, though they may be rebels in the broader societal sense. Because each social system seeks to maintain itself, any person who seriously challenges both the goals and practices of the system will find overwhelming pressures on him, and the odds in favor of his even entering the system are slim.

There is little research to substantiate just how many teachers in a given school or school system would fit into these five categories.[10] Experience suggests that the overwhelming majority of teachers in any given building would have to be labeled "conformists." We must stress that this statement does not mean that *all* teachers behave in the same way or that they are equally effective in implementing the goals and means of the system. On the contrary, conforming to a social system as complex as that of the schools means that one abides by some aspects of it more strictly than by others. We shall find in the conformist group both teachers who are doing a reasonably effective job and those whose students literally climb the walls day in and day out. We shall also find teachers who never deviate from the text, as well as those who seek to introduce some supple-

mentary materials. There are teachers who want to
work closely in the committee structure of the schools,
seeking ways to improve some of the educational practices, and there are also those who would never engage
in such activities. All these characteristics are found
within the pattern of conformity, and we can expect
that most neophyte teachers will find their niche within
this pattern.

We have already suggested that the number of innovators will be very small. In every school in which I
have taught as well as in every school that I have visited,
there has been no evidence to suggest that there are
more than a handful of innovators in any given building. All too frequently, there may be just one or two
people, if that many. One reason for this situation is
that the innovator will find very little support for his
ideas among the majority of his peers. If most teachers
conform to the goals and means of the system, it is not
surprising that they will be unconcerned with the
teacher or administrator who seriously challenges them.
We may suggest that the single most debilitating factor
that limits the potential of the neophyte to improve the
system is the lack of support he will receive from his
colleagues. Not that they will actively oppose him; but
they will show little interest in his work and be unwilling to devote the necessary time to join him. In subtle
but pervasive ways, they will let him know that the
price of leadership is some degree of disassociation from
the pack. The same phenomenon is known in factories
as "don't kill the job." Such language would never be

used among professional teachers, but the effect is much the same.

Although innovators may be rare, each school will have a number of ritualists and retreatists. Most administrators will privately admit that there are two or three teachers on their staffs who they wish could somehow be transferred or removed from the profession. Because ineffectiveness as an educator is rarely a factor in judging a teacher's worth as far as tenure is concerned, most administrators have to learn to live with the ritualists and retreatists. They will be rated unsatisfactory and bounced from school to school, but some of them will remain in the system long enough to get pensions. The principal knows he cannot count on them, and he knows that he has to circumvent them in virtually all his activities. One can only be sympathetic with the administrator who is seeking to encourage his staff when he knows that there are certain individuals on it that are beyond hope.

It is clear that a given teacher may pass from one type of adaptation to another during his career. A teacher who seeks to conform may well become an innovator as he gains experience and insight into ways to improve the means. It is also possible that a teacher who seeks to conform will end up a retreatist or a ritualist or that a teacher who seeks to be an innovator will become so frustrated with attempts to gain a following among his peers or administrative support that he will give up and move into the ranks of conformity—or even into the category of rebellion. The latter is a rare event, but, as we shall discuss in our concluding chapter, it may well be a phenomenon that should be encouraged.

Obviously, research is needed to substantiate the types of adaptation we have outlined. It is also clear that the adaptation of any given individual is affected by such variables as age, sex, social-class origins, and the rigor of prior training. These variations in adaptation are generally accepted by most teachers with whom I have discussed the matter. Too often, however, in discussions of the morale of teachers, the key factor cited is the administrator's impact on the school. Certainly another potent factor, but one not generally acknowledged, is the impact of teachers upon their colleagues in a given building. Innovators will not flourish in a system where conformity is the rule. Some administrators, of course, are themselves dedicated to innovation, and they do all they can to facilitate the work of innovators on their staff. Nonetheless, the overwhelming pressure on the neophyte teacher is toward conformity. Although some variations are permitted within the limits set by the system, to innovate means to cut oneself off to some degree from one's peers and from the system. Few teachers, lawyers, doctors, or assembly workers, are willing to pay this price. It may well be argued that in-service efforts to improve the work of teachers in urban schools have really only two key objectives: to facilitate the work of the innovator and to seek ways to "shake up" the majority of conformists so that they will at least not stand in the way of the innovator, though they themselves may not become actively involved in his work.

As the neophyte teacher begins to see the patterns of adaptation that surround him, he may well be able to control his own pattern of adaptation. The unfortunate fact is that most new teachers are not sensitive to the subtle signs of adaptation that surround them day by day. The elemental fact facing all people concerned with the effectiveness of urban schools is that the vast majority of teachers look upon their work basically as "a job." There is no doubt that there exists a façade of professionalism, that there are many teachers who are indeed professional, and that there are tens of thousands of educators who are seeking to uplift the profession. But many, many teachers are teaching simply because it is a way to earn a living. Although it is dangerous to make this statement, for it is obvious that most people in our society must earn livings, it is also clear that some groups have used the slogan of "professionalism" to hamper efforts to improve the working conditions and salaries of teachers. We are not suggesting, therefore, that "earning a living" is in itself something bad. We are only suggesting that teaching is the type of profession that offers the individual more opportunities to display creativity than do many other occupations in our society. The question is why so few teachers exploit the opportunities to be creative. We have suggested that the system itself is, in a sense, the enemy. Because urban school systems are huge, because they have masses of students and teachers, because they are faced with overwhelming problems, because they are hamstrung by traditions and practices that have encrusted the systems during the last fifty years, the sys-

tem is indeed an enemy. It may also be viewed as a
challenge, but the challenge cannot be grasped unless
we understand the limits the system places on the individual teacher. Nothing we have said should be con-
strued as a "conspiratorial" view of school systems.
There are no groups or individuals within the system,
that is, boards of education or superintendents, who
seek ways to make the system as restrictive as possible
upon the teachers and children within it. There are
some groups outside the system who do seek restrictions, a number of them moving in the tight-lipped
world of the lunatic fringe, the John Birchers and other
101 per cent Americans, for example. There are individuals within the system who are as concerned as is any
excellent teacher about seeking innovative ways to educate children successfully. But boards of education and
superintendents, as well as teachers and principals, are
all part of a system of interrelationships, expectations,
and traditions that press in the direction of conforming
to established molds. These pressures are formidable
and essentially negative in their implications. In other
words, even people who want to help are caught in the
web of the system.

The First Year

Much of what we have discussed so far is summarized
in the often-heard statement that a teacher really learns
his trade in the first year. Some people refer to the first
year of teaching as a test or a trial. There appears to be
widespread agreement among teachers, teacher educa-

tors, and administrators that most of them learned the tasks associated with teaching in the initial months of their careers. Certainly, the experiences of student teaching help to introduce the responsibilities and skills required in teaching. The experience gained in student teaching is usually so limited in scope and obtained under such relatively controlled conditions that the full impact of what it means to be a teacher is not felt. We have already suggested that a teacher must play a number of subroles and that his desire to teach children is only an ideal unless all the other aspects of the job are mastered. Some of the "reality shock" described by Wagenschein can be attributed to the overwhelming pressure of responsibilities and duties that face a teacher every day. Despite attempts at buddy systems and occasional supervision by a principal, a department head, or a supervisor from "downtown," the beginning teacher is generally cut adrift and has to make it on his own in the first year. If team teaching indeed takes hold within the profession, some of the "sink or swim" attributes of the first year will be overcome. But, as team teaching is still largely a slogan rather than a reality, sink or swim is still the rule of thumb.

The beginning teacher has little choice about the order in which he will learn the subroles he must play. From the very first day he must have lessons prepared and activities planned for his students. He must be prepared to manage the group so that if his inchoate skills are challenged he will know how to handle the almost inevitable disturbances that a large class of children can produce. He must learn to fill out and collate the many forms demanded by the bureaucratic structure of the schools. He may quickly learn that collecting milk money may well be the crisis of the day, though he never expected it when he was in teacher training. He must know what to do during an air raid or fire drill; he must know what to do if a child becomes sick in the room; he must learn the 101 rules and regulations of the school so that he can interpret and utilize them as occasion demands.

What should he do when a child is tardy? Should he oppose the automatic rule the school has established, or should he interpret the rule as he believes it should be? What should he do when he cannot find the supplies that his room or class are supposed to have? What should he do when he quickly learns that whatever supplies and mateirals are available are probably not appropriate for the group he is working with? What should he do when, in the middle of a lesson, a message comes from the office requesting a particular bit of information right then and there? How should he handle a parent who comes unexpectedly to the door? How should he handle the requests for lavatory and drinking privileges that beset most elementary school teachers? How should he adjust his personal schedule so that he can catch lunch and still take care of some personal business, because during the school day he will have only a few moments that he can call his own? What should he do about teachers' organizations when the representatives of one or more groups speak to him about joining? How does he acquire audio-visual material? What are the proper forms? Who gets them? Can one depend on delivery?

We do not need to continue listing the types of events and questions that the beginning teacher has. Many of his thoughts and concerns will be about his children, but a great many others will be virtually divorced from his classroom activities. Many of the pressures and anxieties he will feel will be directly related to learning about the system of which he now is a part.

As he becomes acquainted with his colleagues, the neophyte is likely to learn that a good deal of the banter and conversation over lunch or in the smoking room will not be focused on the work of the school or of ways to educate children better. Not that it should be, but he may be dismayed by the frequency of negative reactions of some teachers toward their students and toward teaching as well as by the absence of much support for his efforts. Much of the discussion will focus on topics unrelated either to education or to an examination of teachers' working conditions. As the weeks and months roll by, he will learn that there are certain duties that teachers in his school detest. In most junior and senior high schools, where teachers still are expected to monitor lunch periods, an almost universal dislike of extra duties will be voiced. Whether it be hall duty, lunch duty, or playground duty, there will always be some members of the staff who are unhappy to engage in any of the policing functions of the school, and they will make it known to each and every newcomer to the building for years. He may learn that some teachers feel that the parking space allocated to them is far more important to their professional self-concept than is the textbook they use. He himself may quickly join the complainers if he is in a junior or senior high school and finds that he has five classes a day, in five different rooms, and really has no place that he can call his own. Most schools have completely inadequate facilities for teachers to keep their materials or to meet with students outside of the classroom. If he smokes, he may find, that the boiler room is the only spot in the building where smoking is permitted. He will quickly learn that the faculty will be split on the basis of smokers versus nonsmokers. He will also quickly observe the clique patterns found within any large school. For example, Catholic teachers will very often eat lunch only with other Catholic teachers. In desegregated schools, he may find very little integration among Negro and white teachers. In any large school, divisions by subject area are also very common.

We are not suggesting that the neophyte will not find some teachers who are able to cross subject-area lines, who are able to overcome religious and racial barriers, who will go out of their way to make the neophyte welcome, who are occasionally so excited about some project they are doing that they wish to share it with their colleagues. These individuals exist but, unfortunately, are rather rare. The neophyte will find that a great many of his colleagues care very little about the tasks they are engaged in. If our typology ranging from conformity to rebellion is operating, the neophyte will find that the price of conformity is a rather drab, day-by-day series of contacts with his colleagues. Not that they will be unfriendly or unsympathetic; but we do suggest that teachers in large school systems are as much part of the assembly line of education as are the children passing through the grades. Time and motion studies could very profitably be used in researching the schools. These studies are, of course, abhorrent to educators, for they smack of impersonal, industrial machinations to achieve greater profit. But any realistic examination of the typical school day in an urban school will reveal that the teachers and students alike are on the same treadmill.

The essential problem of curricular reform in public education is that the treadmill, the assembly line, moves along day in and day out at a very regular pace, and it is extremely difficult for teachers and administrators alike to step off that line and to study it in order to find ways to change it. They simply do not have the power to halt the line. Unless they do, all curricular and organizational change will be perfunctory, for it must be imposed on an on-going process. We have already suggested that in some ways schools are very similar to prisons. It is also clear that schools are very much like factories and that model change-over time is long overdue.

We must stress again and again that, for every generalization suggested here, some exceptions do exist. It is possible for the faculty of a given school to become excited about a particular plan of curricular reform and to work together in implementing it. Such prospects, however, are rare. Most educators working on in-service projects are usually not willing to admit that the work-

shops and institutes they conduct involve only handfuls
of people who are willing to be identified as innovators.
In a large high school of 150 faculty members, for example, it is quite possible that a group of teachers will
undertake a particular project in one department. Their
impact on the school and its total operation, however, is
virtually nil. That five or ten teachers out of a large faculty may be engaged in some curricular examination
does not change the facts of life. Not that the efforts of
in-service education should be abandoned. On the contrary, these efforts must continue, but they must also be
analyzed in cold and realistic terms. Any educator who
is satisfied with piddling results will be very satisfied
with the workshop structure that permeates most urban
school systems. Any educator who is concerned about
the fundamental organizational and curricular patterns
of the school and the need for drastic reform can look
upon the workshops that have become common in the
past generation as only tentative beginnings.

The neophyte teacher himself will quickly learn that
almost every major school system does have a continuous series of workshops in which he may participate. As
a neophyte, of course, he will probably feel that he is
not ready for such work; in fact, he will probably be
included only in those in-service activities that are designed to help the neophyte. Most of the other in-
service activities are usually reserved for people who
have established themselves after two or three years. It
will not take long for the neophyte to learn, however,
that the prime goal of any curricular-reform efforts in
which he will take part is a change in the textbooks. On

almost every one of the textbook committees, there may be one person who will suggest that no textbook should be used. His suggestion will be labeled as both good and visionary, "but at this time it would be far wiser to utilize a text." In fact, the people who put down the innovator are probably correct. The majority of teachers would not be able to teach if there were no established text or curriculum guide for their courses. Efforts at even this type of curricular reform are therefore severely hampered.

In short, the neophyte teacher has a great deal to learn in his first year. Mastery of his various roles is an overwhelming task, which, of course varies from school system to school system and from school to school. If the neophyte is part of a small faculty in a small elementary school, very often a feeling of intimacy develops. In every school, however, he will find friends and cohorts to gripe with, to drink beer with, and to enjoy life with. We have not dealt with these types of interpersonal relations, for they are a constant in all professions and occupations. Once he is accepted by his peers, his adjustment to the demands of the job become much easier. We are concerned, however, mainly with the teachers who will accept positions in the large elementary, junior high, and high schools in our cities. They will find that the pressures of mass education are very real and demanding and that they must be mastered if the teacher is to be rated satisfactory. Most educators know that the pressures place an unreasonable demand on the neophyte, for they are unrealistic in terms of the neophyte's meager stock of teaching skills. But very little is done about this problem. We have already noted the buddy system, in which an old-timer is assigned to help out the newcomer, but it is basically a superficial answer to a very pressing problem. Suggestions that the neophyte be treated as an intern, that is, work as part of a team under a master teacher, have borne fruit in some systems, but on the whole the concept has yet to be implemented on a large enough scale really to alter the sink-or-swim alternatives of the first-year teacher. Fortunately, however, internship programs appear to be gaining headway, and the National Teacher Corps has provided an appropriate model for reforming the prevailing system of unreasonable demands on the new teacher. In the National Teacher Corps, for example, a team of interns, under the leadership of an experienced teacher, provides services to the school while each team member is gradually being initiated into the profession. In the main, however, education is the only profession that expects the first-year teacher to exhibit the same skills, judgment, and patience that have been painfully or happily gleaned by the ten-year veteran.

Conclusion

Nowhere is the negative aspect of the system more apparent than in the prevalent attitudes toward children who come from disadvantaged homes. No one intended that school systems should be biased in favor of middle-class children, yet the highest ideal of the system is to work with students who are eager to learn. We are not for a moment suggesting that middle-class children are much more motivated to learn than are lower-class children. There is research, of course, that indicates that this is sometimes true. But even in an all-middle-class school, some teachers will complain about students who are slower than others, who lack interest, who come from broken homes, who stay up late at night, who have to work after school, who are unsupervised, or who do not have a proper diet. These same charges and protestations are made about lower-class children, and there is no doubt that the incidence of many of these problems is higher in inner-city schools than it is in suburban schools. But the crucial fact is that, whether we are talking about an inner-city school serving Negro or Puerto Rican children or a middle-class school serving an all-white community, the curricula, styles of teaching, and restrictions on self-development will be very much the same in both areas. This is the major problem—not so much the backgrounds of the kids as what we are doing to them.

Because many suburban school systems were developed just after World War II and are thus "new," the teacher is more likely to find not only newer buildings but also some of the newer materials and curricular improvements that have been developed over the last twenty years. Any objective study of the so-called "newer curricula," however, will show them to be not much different from the old curricula. The patterns of organization in suburban schools are much the same as those in the older inner-city schools. To the neophyte, suburban schools do offer newer facilities and possibly a smaller class load. More important to many teachers is

the fact that the suburbs offer an opportunity to teach
in all-white, middle-to-lower middle-class areas. The
factor of racial prejudice was noted in Chapter 2, and
its potency should not be underestimated in teacher-
education programs. There is little doubt that most
people entering the teaching profession have made up
their minds about where they would like to teach long
before they have finished student teaching. There is
also little doubt that many universities seeking to recruit and train teachers for the inner city are having
some success. They succeed not because they have an
overwhelming number of applicants for these special
programs, but because they have large student bodies
from which to glean recruits. The majority of college
student are not very interested in the inner city, the
disadvantaged child, or the problems of the urban
school.

This statement is not a condemnation of many university students, for they are not very different from the
body politic, which also has little interest in the problems of the poor. The War on Poverty has been aptly
described as merely a skirmish. The 1960s, which were
to be the most exciting years of the century, are almost
over now, and American society has only begun to resolve its basic inequities—social, economic, and educational. The purpose of our discussion has been to sketch
some of the pressures on the neophyte teacher as he
enters an urban school system. He will feel these pressures whether he is in a suburban or an inner-city area,
whether he is teaching Latin or keeping order in the
homeroom. School systems are far more alike than they

are different. We have often joked about the apocryphal French Minister of Education who claimed that at any given time he could point out the page at which every French teacher would be. We are, as part of our educational folklore, strongly opposed to a national curriculum. Despite our tradition of local autonomy, school curricula have a "sameness" from state to state and region to region. Like it or not, we too have a national curriculum.

The American system of education, as it has evolved, displays more similarities than differences from coast to coast. Because it is a huge system of education it has many variations on the theme, but the theme is essentially the same. It is a lock-step system of education that picks up children at the age of six and processes them to a point at which they either drop out or are graduated somewhere around the age of sixteen or seventeen. It is a mass system of education, and, despite all the protestations of reaching the individual, it produces a mass product. There is no doubt that it has many, many strengths. It is puerile to dwell on these strengths at this juncture, for even with its strengths, there is good reason to insist that the system must be improved. To argue that it is the best system in the world is also futile. It is better than some, and it certainly is adapted to our goals as a nation; but this does not mean that it can not be improved or that its improvement is not essential.

All the debate and efforts over the last five years to find ways to improve urban schools have yet to bear fruit. We have merely scratched the surface in examining patterns of organization, time allocations, staff allocations, materials, and approaches that must be altered if we are to do the job well. The fact that we are at least debating the problem and seeking to do something about it is hopeful. The message of this chapter, as gloomy as it may appear to some, is not at all a pessimistic one. The literature on the disadvantaged child has already well characterized their needs, the types of teachers we need to fulfill these needs, and the kinds of organizational change that must be achieved. Our concern has been to suggest to the neophyte teacher that, when he enters the school, whether it be in an urban or suburban setting, he will be expected to conform to the system in each and every way. If the neophyte understands this demand and recognizes that it does not mean capitulation, there is some hope that a new breed of teachers will yet be achieved.

We turn next to the experiences of several people who have taught or administered in urban school settings. Their experiences will help to exemplify the line of reasoning we have been discussing. They will also introduce us to several other dimensions of teaching in urban schools.

Notes

1. Dorothy McGeoch, *et al.*, *Learning to Teach in the Urban School* (New York: Teachers College Press, 1965), p. 1.
2. *Cf.* Harold L. Hodgkinson, *Education in Social and Cultural Perspectives* (Englewood Cliffs, N. J.: Prentice-Hall, 1962), Chapter 2.
3. Patricia Cayo Sexton, *Education and Income* (New York: Viking, 1961), pp. 277–9.

4. Erving Goffman, "The Characteristics of Total Institutions," in Amitai Etzioni, ed., *Complex Organizations: A Sociological Reader* (New York: Holt, 1964).

5. Mortimer Kreuter, "The Teacher in the Brown Paper Bag," *The Urban Review* (May 1966), n. p.

6. Willard Waller, *The Sociology of Teaching* (New York: Wiley, 1965), p. 103.

7. Robert J. Havighurst and Bernice L. Neugarten, *Society and Education* (3rd ed.; Boston: Allyn & Bacon, 1967), Chapter 17.

8. For an historical analysis of the interrelationship between the industrial ethic of efficiency and the schools, see Raymond E. Callahan, *Education and the Cult of Efficiency* (Chicago: University of Chicago Press, 1962).

9. Robert K. Merton, *Social Theory and Social Structure* (rev. ed., New York: Free Press, 1957), Chapter 4.

10. *Cf.* Ronald G. Corwin, *A Sociology of Education* (New York: Appleton, 1965), pp. 257–63. Using another typology, Corwin estimates the number of rebels within the system at 10 per cent.

An Inside View

To elaborate on our discussion of some of the dynamics the neophyte teacher may encounter in joining the faculty of an urban school, we turn now to the insights of several people with first-hand experience in inner-city schools. Experience in itself is not a credential for objectively reporting the complex social mechanisms of the school. Anthropologists have recorded the difficulty for even trained participant-observers of controlling their value judgments. It is also possible that experience can dull one's perceptions as one becomes conditioned to the system. Or, as some wag has put it, some teachers with thirty years of experience have really had only one year multiplied by thirty. Yet there is little doubt that the newcomer to any field can benefit by exposure to the first-hand accounts of more experienced personnel.

Research into the key variables associated with teaching success in urban schools is, at best, fragmentary. Even if it were definitive, the literature on the disadvantaged needs all the autobiographical material that can be acquired. Autobiographical material offers a sense of immediacy that contributes to involvement in the ideas presented. Oscar Lewis' writings on the culture of poverty are a case in point. In education, it is evident that teachers' attitudes toward the disadvantaged are the key intervening variable. That is, no matter what the program or technique proposed for inner-city schools, how teachers view their children makes or breaks the new approach, and it is in autobiographical, first-hand accounts that attitudinal factors are most likely to be demonstrated. Autobiographical material is needed from children themselves as well as from competent individuals working with children. The accounts recorded here represent the latter source. Although case studies have heuristic limitations, the following examples ring true in our ears, and, though they are all drawn from one large school system, the situations described are essentially universal in American urban education.

We turn first to a teacher who recounts her experiences during her first year in an inner-city school. She does not dwell on her adjustment to the system but does suggest some of the fear many new teachers feel when they are assigned to "taboo areas." Her concern is mainly with her metamorphosis *vis-à-vis* her students. Not many beginning teachers are as perceptive or as candid as she in analyzing their thoughts, goals, and reactions. This teacher's insights and self-awareness are apparent even in the title of her essay:

Socialization:
A White Teacher Grows Up
in an Inner-City School

by HAZEL KARBEL

Socialization can be defined as a process by which the individual learns the ways of a society within a particular culture. If we accept the premise that the school is a separate culture within our broader culture, I even submit that each teacher must go through the socialization process anew upon entering a particular school. If a teacher does not become socialized to his new environment, he will never truly understand his students. Without this understanding, he will never bring about change.

Each teacher brings himself to a particular school. Although this may sound redundant, it is the key to all that will happen to that teacher while he is in a particular school. Each teacher will apply his former experiences, prejudices, stereotypes, and morality, as well as that unknown "personality," to each new situation within the school. The extent to which a teacher will adjust or change his attitudes to fit the needs of a school and its student body is greatly influenced by background and personality.

Although I was born in the small town of Peekskill,

New York, with a population of 22,000, I had an unusually enlightened upbringing, considering what a typical middle-class upbringing in such a community usually is. My parents were liberal Jews in a town of few Jews, let alone liberal ones. Furthermore, they did not practice their religion, which made both Jew and Gentile suspect them of being strange. They always voted Democratic or independent in an overwhelmingly Republican community. My father was an amateur musician and a music lover, a hobby shared by few of the townspeople. He never cared about making money; consequently, we never were well off. But there was always money for records, books, music lessons, dancing lessons, magazines, and concerts. Education was highly valued.

I grew up in an atmosphere of great freedom of thought. No topic was considered too "touchy" to be openly discussed. Such causes as civil rights were always championed by my parents, who always were on the side of the underdog.

I had no Negro or Oriental friends; there were none in my school. We attended a rural public school on the outskirts of the town. The Negro families all resided within the city limits and their children attended the Peekskill schools. I never felt any racial prejudice. This was due to the fact that my parents knew interracial couples who lived in New York City, only fifty miles away, and my parents' attitude in such matters was always very liberal. Such terms as "communistic," "anarchistic," and "socialistic" were common, as my parents knew many people who could fall into all three categories.

Notwithstanding all this liberality of thought, I led a fairly sheltered life in other ways. I never saw great poverty except when riding by it on the subways in New York. My friends came from typically middle-class backgrounds, and I grew up with the educational goals and aspirations of most middle-class children. I "knew" that I was going to college from the time I was eight or nine years old. I "knew" I'd be a teacher from that same moment. A teacher, to me, was a respected person; a person who could "teach" children, be looked up to by students and by parents, and whose word should not be questioned. A teacher was also an independent person who could earn a decent living.

The University of Michigan was my training ground as well as my "hunting" ground. I became a teacher and met my husband in four years. Marriage changed my plans somewhat in that I had always expected to live in the East. Instead of going back to New York, I wound up in Detroit. My new family, a highly respected upper-middle class Jewish family, had been Detroiters for half a century. When I accepted a teaching position at —— Junior High School, I was at once regarded as heroic, insane, foolish, and daring by my many relatives and friends. More than once I was warned to "leave school before dark" and to not return until morning. I often heard such questions as: "Are they really human?" "Can they really learn?" "Aren't you afraid to teach them?" I found that I was becoming somewhat of a *cause célèbre* among my generation of friends, who viewed me as some brave, white Joan of Arc going into battle each day against a giant black army. I was and am neither brave nor cowardly, but during the first few months at —— I may have felt that I was one or both.

The nature of a community largely determines what goes on in school. To attempt to separate school from community is to engage in unrealistic thinking. A school and its community are inseparable. (James Conant, *Slum and Suburbs*, 1961)

Not being a native Detroiter, I had enough trouble finding the school. It was not until much later that I realized
the importance of the quotation cited above. Only then did
I begin to explore the neighborhood, through books as well
as by personal contact with the neighborhood and its inhabitants. It is a highly transient neighborhood with families
leaving for many of the following reasons: eviction due to
failure to pay rent; hope to find work elsewhere; having saved
enough money to move to higher-income neighborhoods.
People move into the neighborhood for lack of funds to go
elsewhere. Rural southerners, both Negro and white, move to
the neighborhood in hope of finding jobs and earning more
than they could in the South. Between 1950 and 1960, the
percentage of Negroes living in the South dropped from
60 to 52 per cent. Many of these Negroes settled in north-
ern cities like Detroit for the purpose of bettering their lot.
Unfortunately, jobs for the unskilled laborer are often hard
to come by. The men who do work often earn less than
their wives. Women, in general, are able to earn fairly good
wages. Therefore, some men would rather not work than
have their wives earn more. The streets always have a few
unemployed men who hang around and prey on girls. Many
girls complain that their greatest problem is getting from
school to their apartments without being molested in the
hallway. Often the adult males are not harmful, but they
fail to inspire emulation. Civic responsibility does not exist
to a great degree. The majority of the occupants do not
accept responsibility for the immediate community. Certain grass-roots organizations are beginning to arise in the
neighborhood, but these do not attract a large percentage
of the community. Many families with whom I have talked
do not consider themselves part of the neighborhood; thus
they wish to have no part in anything which will connect

them with the neighborhood. They claim that they are
merely biding their time until they save enough to move
elsewhere. This was evident in a home call I made.

When I arrived at the apartment of the R. family, the
first thing I noticed was the spotless condition of the
crowded five-room flat. The R. family consists of six children, ranging in age from three years to seventeen. The
five school age children are all in school and are good students. The father is a factory worker, the mother a house-
wife. They are hard-working people, people who have a
definite contribution to make to any community. But they
participate little in community affairs. They rarely get to
visit their children's teachers, and, since their children do
well in school, they are never forced to come to school to
discuss discipline problems. One of the R. children is in
my homeroom and has been for a year and a half. I decided
it was time to meet her parents, and I managed to get an
invitation to visit the apartment one day after school. It
was during the course of this visit that I realized why many
of the more articulate members of this community were not
participating in community affairs. Mrs. R. complained to
me about the crowded conditions under which her family
was now living. Then she said, "But we will be moving to
our own home next year." One of the children yelled,
"Next year. That's what you said last year!" Mrs. R. explained that since they had moved from the South, they
had been saving to buy a house in the suburbs. I asked
her when the family had made this move, thinking that it
must have been within the last two years. "Eight years
ago," Mrs. R. answered.

The student body at ―― Junior High School is made
up of children whose family backgrounds vary greatly.

However, even in the best family situations in the neighborhood, there are problems. Ideally the family provides for the physical, emotional, and intellectual well-being of the child to the level of understanding and aspiration which will support the school. But these foundations are often lacking in the disadvantaged child. My visit to Denice's home made this very clear to me. Reading material in most homes is nonexistent. When many children leave school they never see anyone read anything, not even a newspaper. Many of the parents are practically illiterate. They have low occupational and educational objectives for their children. They are often apathetic and indifferent to their children's successes or failures, and they pass this apathy on to their children. Yet many of these children have ability levels which indicate they could perform better than average in school and life achievement.

For example, Denice was a belligerent member of my homeroom. She was always getting into trouble for "sassing" her teachers. She refused to cooperate with me in matters such as bringing absence notes, returning report cards, and other matters of record-keeping which plague every other homeroom teacher. Finally, I decided that the only way I was going to get Denice's report card back in time to mark it (she had had it at home for four weeks) was to pick it up myself. Denice was not very happy to learn that I was to take her home that afternoon. We arrived at her house, in the low-rise section of a public housing project, and once again she asked me not to come in. I had already called her mother to arrange the visit, so I was determined to keep my appointment.

This was one of my first visits to the projects, and I was revolted, appalled, and saddened by what I saw. The downstairs consisted of two rooms, a kitchen and a living room. The kitchen was filthy; dishes piled high in the sink, food covered the table, stove, and the floor. Everything was covered with grease. The living room was in the same condition. The furniture consisted of a worn-out couch, one chair, and a large television set. Her mother was sleeping on the couch, the television set was blaring, and six little boys, ranging in ages from three to ten, were running around screaming and yelling. The children were dressed in rags and were no cleaner than their surroundings. Mrs. ——— awoke, and we began to talk about Denice, who had run upstairs to fetch her report card. Denice had failed three subjects, and, when I mentioned to her mother that her conduct was not much better, her mother commanded Denice to return to the room. "Get me the strap," was all her mother said. Amidst the laughter of the little boys, the strap was brought. "If a teacher ever has to come with you again, you are gonna be sorry." Her mother then assured me that Denice would give me no more trouble. "As soon as you leave, she's gonna get a whippin'." The girl just stood still throughout all of this and said nothing. I thanked her mother for her cooperation and left, feeling that I'd done more harm to this girl by visiting her home than if I'd never seen her mother or her home. And yet I knew why Denice was belligerent. I knew now why she did poorly in her school work. This visit had opened my eyes to the reality that many students like Denice face each day when they leave the unreality of the school.

Fear is the major reason why many young teachers do not accept appointments to city schools. They are afraid they will be trapped in a "blackboard jungle"; they are afraid of physical attack; they are afraid that they cannot deal with the situations they will meet in the schools. . . . (Harry Rivlin, *Teachers for Our Big City Schools*, 1965, p. 9)

This is precisely the way I felt about accepting a position in a "bad" neighborhood. Had I been living in New York City, where I am more familiar with the names of the "bad" neighborhoods, I probably never would have accepted a position similar to the one I accepted at —— J.H.S. Neither my liberal background, attitude, nor college courses had prepared me to cope with my feelings of panic when my first class walked into my first classroom. To begin with, all my teaching experience up to the moment had been with seventh graders, most of whom were smaller than I was. This class consisted of ninth graders, ranging in ages from fourteen to sixteen. They were young people, but in my mind they were large, dark threats. I purposely used the word "dark," because the color of their skin, for the first time in my life, made me afraid. They were different. They belonged here, and I was the outsider.

I began the class in a shaky manner, and everything was going along fine; that is, the students sat and stared at me quietly. Suddenly, in walked Willie. The class perked up quite a bit. Willie was notorious, I later learned. He was almost sixteen, the age when the junior high can legally bounce its students, or when its students can legally quit. Both school and student seemed to be biding their time. Willie was a Negro boy of about 5 feet 8 inches tall. He was wearing a gray suit, skin tight pants and jacket, pink shirt, and pointed black boots. His hair had been processed. I couldn't tell which was worse—his brand of cologne or the slight traces of liquor on his breath. While I stood helplessly by, Willie greeted all his friends and then consented to sit down.

After that first meeting, Willie rarely showed up in class. Mondays seemed to be his day set aside for school. After three such Mondays had come and gone, I learned my first lesson about Willie and other "Willies" I would later meet. He was bright. He could read well, had a beautiful handwriting, and could express himself adequately on paper and orally. But I also learned from his records and the guidance counselor that his two brothers were in prison for robbery, he had no father, he drank, and had been in trouble with the police several times. Willie dropped out of school for good after a few more Mondays. Neither I nor anyone else in the school system had ever been able to reach him.

The remainder of the class was far less spectacular. But they had me cowed, and they knew it. They set up the unwritten rules for classroom procedure, and I followed them. For example, each day all the boys came late to class. They came from swimming and their excuse was "We don't have enough time to shower and dress." When I tried to put an end to this, they raised such a fuss that I chose what I thought to be the easier way out: I let them have their way. Many of these same boys, and girls as well, never brought a pencil or a sheet of paper to class. The school policy regarding supplies had never been explained to me. I didn't want to go to the counselor for help for fear of being thought incompetent or some such thing. Furthermore, I felt that I could at least help these "poor deprived youngsters" by lending them supplies. They invariably lost the paper, since they had no looseleafs to keep it in, and they forgot to return the pencils unless I specifically reminded them to do so. It was not until later that I learned that most of them had supplies in their lockers and were just not taking the trouble to bring them to class. Why should they? I had made it too easy for them to borrow what they needed. They arrived in class, left class, and what happened in-between was inconsequential.

Their apathy made me believe that they were incapable.

Their attitude and my pity for them caused me to demand less and less from them. Thus I received less and less from them. It took me three months to begin to change all of my attitudes and approaches, but with this class it was really too late.

A year later I met one of the class members, a quiet girl who was absent a great deal but who was one of the few students willing to make up any work she had missed. She was currently enrolled in high school. She expressed surprise to learn that I was still at the school. "I never thought you'd stick it out," she said. "I used to feel so sorry for you. The kids really took advantage of you. They knew you were afraid of us."

That first semester was an education for me. I not only dealt with ninth graders, but eighth graders as well. On the second day of the term, the first full school day, I had to take my eighth-grade group to lunch. Lining them up seemed to be something easily done, I thought. The class got in line; I started to get my purse when, the next thing I knew, I was a spectator at a violent fight. Two boys were on the floor, one with his hands on the other's neck, was banging the latter's head on the floor. Once again I was the outsider. I was outside the cheering ring of spectators which had instantly formed around the boys. I sent someone to the office for help, and a male counselor came and broke up the fight. I couldn't eat lunch that day. My hands were shaking so badly I had a difficult time holding a cup of coffee. I still hate to see a fight, but I am far more equipped to handle one than I was on that day.

My last class of the day was also an eighth-grade group. This group was made up of some of the brightest eighth graders in the school, some of whom are now attending a school for advanced students and are being tested for pri-

vate prep school enrollment. But my attitude toward them
was influenced by what had occurred in my other classes. I
feared, at times hated and misunderstood, many of my
students at various times. I felt frustrated that they could
not or would not do the homework I gave them or pass the
tests I gave them. Rather than try to find a new approach,
I felt that they just couldn't learn.

I went home at night thoroughly exhausted just from
trying to maintain order. Dealing with pupils like Ida didn't
help to increase my self-confidence. Ida was tall, physically mature, and fifteen. She was in the eighth grade.
"Spontaneous" might be the way to describe Ida's behavior. At any time she might burst into song, tears, shouts, or
laughter. That she would stay in her seat, especially when
she was upset, could not be relied upon. At times she
would ask me if I thought she was "queer." The other
class members accused me many times of being afraid of
Ida. Once I punished a boy for something and he blurted
out, "Why don't you ever punish Ida for that? We all
think you're scared of her. You're scared she'll beat you
up." I denied it, but, truthfully, I was afraid of this girl.

Georgette and Theodore were two students whose ambition, drive, and brainpower could take them anywhere.
When they became discipline problems, I realized that all
of my trouble must not be entirely the students' fault. One
day I allowed the class to tell what was wrong. "What
would you like to do in here?" I asked them. I knew that
this could be suicide for me. I was putting myself in the
hands of my students. But I was desperate. They told me.
One after another, the more vociferous members of the
class made it quite clear that they were bored. Georgette's
words have stayed with me: "Why can't we ever study
anything of great importance? Why can't our class work

be fun? Why can't we discuss problems about civil rights? The work is too easy. I have never been so bored in my life." Before dismissing the class that day, I told them that I would try to use their suggestions in planning my lessons for the remainder of the term.

At home that evening, I felt shattered. I was deeply hurt. My ego had been wounded, yet I knew that I had to stop being hurt and start doing something. Much of what these eighth graders had said was all too true. If the cause for my change in attitude and approach must be pinpointed to any special time, I would say that this event was the catalyst. I realized that to salvage myself and my students, I had to look immediately and carefully at curriculum, rules and punishments, my fears, my expectations, and my goals, as well as my methods of introducing and handling all of these areas. I had to come to terms with all the Theodores, Georgettes, and Idas as well. I had to find out about the neighborhood, the families, and the surroundings of my students. This was my beginning.

I had to get the children interested and I had to get them to want to learn. It meant a lot of hard work. It meant after-school hours spent creating new materials, searching for materials, and then wondering if all of this was going to work in the classroom. It meant devising new ways of motivating a class. I first learned to capture the attention of the class. Once I had it, I could try to channel it in the direction I wished it to go. But this is an everyday struggle. Each day the attention of the students must be courted and won anew and then centered on a certain task.

While raising my aspirations for my students, I also had to realize that some children who tried hard could not and would not ever receive an "A" or a "B" if the standard teaching procedures of read, write, and recite were followed. A variety of new tasks had to be devised in which all students could find some degree of success and feel some sense of accomplishment and pride. Of course, I am well aware that none of these things are "new," but to me at that time they could be considered as such.

In the area of punishment for breaking rules, I had a lot to learn. I was unsuccessful in applying the "protracted reasoning and arguing about rules and regulations that is so popular in modern homes, but is most ineffective with the disadvantaged child who has had little of this type of experience" (Frank Riessman, *The Culturally Deprived Child*, New York: Harper, 1962, p. 47). As I got to know the parents of my students, I soon learned that punishment took two common forms—physical or deprivation of privileges. This pattern could easily be imitated, while excluding the use of corporal punishment. I now set up a list of classroom rules and regulations. I let the class know about these rules. I also listed the punishments that would be incurred if any rules were broken. I tried to keep the loss of privileges as closely related to the "crime" as possible. If, for example, a child ran, screamed, or poked others on the way to lunch, he or she might lose the privilege of going to lunch with the class for a day or two. This type of punishment is usually quite effective.

My personal attitude toward my students had to change or any other changes would not be enacted effectively. I previously had pitied, feared, and loved some of my students. The more I worked with these children, the more my fear abated. Their hair, clothes, and skin all began to assume the proper proportions. Furthermore, as Frank Riessman had written:

While underprivileged children strongly desire physical warmth, it would be a mistake to believe that they want intense affection. . . . Deprived children need respect rather than "love" from their teacher. . . . Love is not a major issue in the deprived home; it is not used as a discipline technique, and the child generally does not feel that he must win love or that he can lose it. Respect, on the other hand, is something that the child is not likely to have received in the culture at large. . . . He needs a teacher who will stand by him, someone on whom he can depend. For him to be accepted despite his initial hostility is paramount. (*Ibid.*, pp. 46–7)

As I began to acquaint myself with my students, I noticed how eager they were to have me prove that I could be trusted. I had to prove this to them or all my reforms in areas of curriculum and classroom management would be meaningless. Some way of proving this came about naturally. I noticed that, when I would drive to school or leave school with a Negro teacher who lived near me the students would take notice. Invariably they would ask me where he lived and where I lived. When they learned that there were Negroes living in my building, they were silent yet gradually became more open about their homes and families. One day I took my entire homeroom to see my apartment. I live in a three-room apartment in a new, integrated area of the city. The manager looked rather amazed to see thirty-five adolescents of all shapes and sizes pile through the door followed by their teacher. But he said nothing. The children, on the other hand, were bursting with questions: "Are you really going to take us into your apartment?" "Won't anyone mind?" "How much does it cost to live here?" I answered each question and many others as I observed their reactions to actually seeing my home. One little girl asked, "Do they let Negroes live in the building?" I said that they did. Someone else said, "You're lucky!"

For weeks after that I noticed a tremendous change in my relationship with my homeroom students. They constantly talked about the experience: the elevators, the building, my books, records, furniture, and me. They would do almost anything I asked. Cooperation was at a peak between students and teacher. They bragged to many of their friends that their teacher had taken them to her house. They began inviting me to their homes to meet their families. These visits have been invaluable in terms of building rapport with students and their parents. As a teacher of children, rather than a teacher of English or social studies, I realized that one must know the child before attempting to teach him anything. To try to teach English before understanding the nature of the child you are trying to reach is a waste of time.

In one of my seventh-grade classes this past semester, my students were writing compositions entitled "The Power" and what they'd do if they had it. "The Power" was the ability to wish anything or say anything and have it come true immediately. When the children completed their essays, I asked for volunteers to read their work aloud. One boy got up and read a lengthy account of what he'd do to his homeroom teacher, a very strict, elderly woman, who has the reputation of being "mean." Eventually he'd killed her off and all the girls in the class. I was the only female person left. As a matter of fact, I was the last to get the proverbial ax. At this point I realized that my socialization was paying off. I had been able to enact two out of three stages necessary in teaching these children. The first stage is building rapport (being accepted). The second is when your own excitement and fascination with a topic spreads to the children, so that they want to tackle a certain job because of your interest in it. The third and last stage is one in which the child begins to feel his own power and begins to realize what he can do with knowledge, sees the value of his own ideas. This may happen with only a few children. I am still striving to achieve this stage.

I consider myself lucky. I managed to overcome the cultural barrier at stage one and was able to achieve the rapport which is absolutely necessary before moving to stage two, the learning stage. Most teachers who leave the inner city do not effectively reach stage one, nor do they believe it is possible to do so. To keep these and other teachers in the inner city, it is necessary to "socialize" teachers before they have completed their teacher training. They must see teachers working with the disadvantaged, not just at stage two or three but at stage one as well. If teachers are not socialized before entering a difficult teaching situation, there will always be a shortage of qualified teachers in the very schools where good teachers are sorely needed.

* * *

Charles H. Cooley's looking-glass self is well demonstrated in this account of one teacher's sensitive response to her students. Step by step, our new teacher learned all the exhuberant and subtle means by which students let a teacher know that they trust him and respond to him. The concept of socialization is also very appropriate here. All newcomers to the social system of the school must learn how to survive within that system, and adjustments to the children are indeed crucial. It is a subtle learning process that all teachers must experience. Other adjustments are just as demanding.

One of the major adjustments has been stressed throughout our discussions, that is, working relationships with one's peers. Although the following article is merely an introduction to the complex network of interpersonal factors at work on a school faculty, our writer goes right to the point.

———————————

Faculty Dynamics
and the
Neophyte Teacher

by ERLENE FLOWERS

If anyone who teaches would conceive of the school setting as a stage and could divorce his mind from the situation and remove it to a point right outside of the wings, he would find a situation that is so comic in nature that it could run in an off-Broadway theater for at least a decade. Each act would be different, and once divorced from it the teacher would realize that nothing short of monkeys at play is as comic as the school setting and the interplay between the people involved.

It is into a situation like that in which I find myself that neophytes are allowed the privilege of charging full speed ahead without being forewarned by anybody. The college of education, for example, does not teach the mechanics of collecting bookstore money, books, materials, and supplies. It leaves the neophyte teacher open to be disillusioned, disregarded, and often disqualified by the people in the profession who must rate him. Often nothing more is really wrong than that the neophyte does not understand soon enough where the power lies in a building. Somewhere along the line in the college of education, somebody should be designated to do some real "down to earth" reasoning with the neophyte as to what to really expect on the job.

I had always held with the premise that a school's faculty has a lot to do with the formation of the personality and spirit of a new teacher. I strongly believe that the success or failure of a neophyte teacher depends a great deal upon his reception into a school in the first six or eight weeks of teaching. Further, I have always held that the power structure of a school may not always be where it has been properly delegated by the board of education. Often, I think, when the informal power structure is radically different from the delegated authority, faculty dynamics become so confused that they affect the quality of teaching in a building.

Six years ago, I began as an elementary specialist in art education under a principal who was one semester from retirement. The assistant principal at the time was young, ambitious, and ulcerous. I was twenty-one years old, fresh out of college, and fresh from three hypothetical student-teaching contacts that had supposedly prepared me for a career in education. Teachers, in my eyes, *were* extremely professional guardians of educational truth. I am relating all this to say that in the six weeks that followed *Up the Down Staircase* had nothing on me.

I was so bothered by my first six weeks as a teacher that I thought I would resign. I was treated so badly by the

"pseudoprofessionals" that I had previously admired that
I sat in a local bar with a friend and literally cried my eyes
out. I still remember my "good buddy" from the school
down the street, who saved my career in teaching that day.
I think that it is also because of him that I was able to
develop into one of the stronger teachers in the building. I
would like to share his advice with you:

> Quit? Quit? Don't be a fool! Be realistic, my dear, come
> to Papa and let him tell you something you obviously
> don't know. One, you are now in a profession, and I
> use the term loosely, that is filled with the most petty,
> scared, old, and uncreative individuals in the world. Two,
> *you* are *young* and not to be trusted. You have *new*
> methods and *new* ideas. Don't be misled, my dear, the
> profession fights these at every turn. Three, don't be
> afraid of him [the principal]. *Smile* and invite the old coot
> in. Call the old girl [the art supervisor] before they do
> and tell her the problem that you have told me. She's a
> finky old witch, *but* she has a helluva ear. Believe me
> when I say make a friend of her. Blow her up [tell her
> how great she is]. You'll need her to survive. Believe me,
> sweetie, most of the teachers in the building don't trust
> you for several reasons, one of the most important of
> which is that you are *creative*. The old girl understands
> this. Lastly, little girl, get your chin up off your chest.
> These old bats with their old philosophies and old ways
> *have* to retire some day. Just see to it that *you* don't
> ever become as petty as they are. *Stay* with it. Someday
> there will be enough like us to rock the boat. Maybe we
> really can make it a *profession*.

It is a long speech, but believe me when I say that, if it
had not been for my philosopher buddy, I would have
said, "Shove it!" Many times afterward I have had to tell
myself: "They will retire. It has got to get better." I have
passed this speech along to several younger teachers who
had seemed to have reached their wits' end.

* * *

Again, we are sharing only one teacher's experiences, but the feeling of being hemmed in, of being "routinized," of being restricted in both open and subtle ways is apparent. Not that this teacher has not found supportive individuals in her work; but the initial and overwhelming pressure has been toward conforming to the system. Not enough teacher educators and school-system supervisors are aware of how hard the first weeks on the job can be, and our contributor was lucky to have a "good buddy" to counsel her. However one may react to the advice, the fact remains that teaching is hard work, and it takes a strong individual to adjust to the demands of the job without being dismayed by some of the people in the system who tend to look negatively at the new teacher and his "new ideas."

Our next selection touches on the behavior of some high school youth, but its major emphasis is on the routines of a day on the job. Our contributor was a social-studies department head in a large high school, with more than ten years' experience in the system. He begins by outlining a typical day. As in the previous selection his comments on some of the nitty-gritty details of the teacher's day are especially revealing. No one ever tells the neophyte that he may well have to "cover" for an absent teacher on a "flu day." No one ever suggests that there are slip-ups on the delivery of films. Yet these minor incidents soon begin to make the difference between a "good day" and a "bad day," regardless of how well things may have gone with one's students. Appropriately enough, our typical day begins in the office, which for most teachers is the first stop of the morning.

Views of
a Department Head
by ARNOLD GLOVINSKY

The day begins with a stop at the main office—to accomplish four main objectives. First, to pick up mail and messages at the mail box. Second, to check the list of absent teachers for the day. Third, to scan the bulletin board for notices and announcements, especially for reminders of reports *due today*. And fourth, to spend a few minutes just socializing and picking up bits of information—fact and rumor—typical of every school.

Of the four reasons for checking in at the office, the most important to the department head, is unquestionably to discover which teachers are absent for the day. Not only am I concerned with my own department, but others as well. An absent teacher means waiting for the substitute, who often arrives after the first class has begun, and frequently after the first class has ended. There are times, especially during the winter and early spring, when the "flu" is endemic, when there are so many teachers out that substitutes in sufficient numbers are not available.

I noted that I was concerned with absenteeism not only

in my own department. Often a teacher in a different subject area would have one or two classes to teach in social studies. This need to "round out a program" would most often afflict the physical education department, so an absent gym teacher could result in social studies classes not being "covered."

If a counselor is not present, his regular replacement might be a social-studies teacher, with a call going out for a social-studies substitute. Here again it is a matter of "covering" classes.

What is done during the first class period depends largely on whether substitutes have arrived. I would take one class, and sometimes two if the rooms were adjacent. If there were no teacher, I would send the class to study halls. And on occasion, although it was contrary to the rules, I would meet a class, get it started on an assignment, and leave, notifying the teacher on hall duty nearest the room, asking him to keep open an eye and an ear.

Now that the day has begun and the question of substitutes has been settled, the day settles into an hour by hour progression.

My office is shared with two other department heads and two teachers. My desk is usually cluttered with announcements of new tests, periodicals, films, filmstrips, records, and other teaching materials. Much of the advertising copy is addressed to the principal, who in turn routes it to me if it relates to social studies.

Since we are building our library of filmstrips and phonograph records, my collection of catalogs of available audio-visual materials is extensive. When new brochures arrive, I circulate them among teachers in the department. If reactions are favorable, we order on approval or for preview. Money comes from our department fund, which is maintained through the collection from each student of a five-cent social-studies fee.

It might be expected that teachers in the department would demonstrate intense interest in acquiring audio-visual aids—to have filmstrips and records available to them with virtually no advanced reservation or waiting period needed. With few exceptions, however, such is not the case. For a number of reasons, which I shall discuss later, most teachers do not make good use of the materials available to them.

When a motion picture is scheduled for showing in a large room to which classes can be brought, the response is fairly good. Of course, this requires little or no preparation. Further, it is seldom that the teacher has had the opportunity to preview the film; the exigencies of scheduling and the press of other duties ordinarily militate against knowing what to expect. If a teacher brings a second or third class to see the film on the same day (frequently the film is run every period), it is possible to spend at least a short time in properly introducing it.

But far better than the mass viewing of a motion picture, which may or may not coincide with the subject matter the class happens to be studying on that particular day, are the other audio-visual materials available which can be made to fit precisely the needs of a class during a specific period. Why are they not used more often? First, it is difficult to overcome established teaching patterns. Like everyone else, teachers tend to resist change, and to continue in the ways they know best. If in the past they have taught their American history classes the causes of the American Revolution by listing on the chalkboard the Intolerable Acts, then the chances are they will continue to do so, even though the impact on students of such a method is negligible. The use of other materials requires a reassessment of method, and most of us are not prone to do so.

Secondly, and this is truly a paradox, teachers feel pressured to "cover" materials. How can they complete a required course of study if they "lose" time by playing a record containing music and songs of the Revolutionary period? How can they complete the course if they "lose" time by showing pictures of the people and events the class is studying? I fear our obsession with the chronological presentation of subject matter stands in the way of creative teaching. Apparently there is a greater concern over "moving along" than there is with examining the conceptual framework within which an academic discipline can begin to be understood by high-school students. And it is not that we ignore this problem in our department meetings. Time and again we have discussed, and agreed, I believe, on the need to achieve a balance between "moving along" and "completing the course" as against taking the time to develop ideas, broad concepts, and the "feel" of the subject. The two are not mutually exclusive, but how difficult it is to overcome inertia, to change the way we perceive the job of teaching.

Thirdly, we simply talk too much. We still function on the level of "Now, you listen while I explain and you learn." We know that somehow pupils must become actively involved, and yet we seem to spend most of our time talking at pupils, rather than to and with them. This is especially wasteful in inner-city schools. I am convinced that after a few minutes of being talked at the boys and girls simply tune us out. The more sophisticated appear to be listening intently. Those who cannot play the game as well will fidget and actively display their disinterest. Occasional questions from the teacher rarely bring enlightened response. Much of this results from having been "tuned out"; but not all, for there are other factors at play.

A visitor on his first trip to an inner-city high school is often surprised at what he observes. Acquainted with the blackboard-jungle syndrome, he expects to find teachers struggling to achieve and maintain at least a small degree of classroom order. He has been prepared to see leering, unruly, loud exhibitionists misbehaving in ways that make teaching impossible. Instead, the visitor is likely to find the class *behaving* in ways that make the usual teaching methods impossible.

For the class is not unruly; it is not loud; it is not filled with leering exhibitionists. On the contrary, the class is orderly, quiet, and filled with many who do not wish to be seen. The problem turns out not to be one of noise, but of silence. The voice you hear is the teacher's, talking at the pupils, seeking a spark of understanding, seeing the same few hands go up to respond to a question, or to give an opinion, or (wonder of rare wonders) to ask a question which is not procedural.

This lack of response, I am convinced, is not because so few know the answer or have no contributions to make. Rather, it stems from a peculiarity of the inner-city high-school student. The psychological and sociological forces which have molded him require that he protect himself at all times. The world is hostile, school is hostile, the teacher is hostile. If he answers a question or makes a judgment, he has let down his defenses and becomes vulnerable. Experience has taught him that it is better not to volunteer an answer, for the answer may be wrong. To be wrong is to risk censure. Better not say anything—remain invulnerable—say "I don't know," and let the teacher pass on to someone else.

So, unorthodox as it may seem, the successful inner-city high-school teacher will of course seek the "right" answer, but he will also cherish the wrong answer. He will not fawningly and artificially complement the pupil who is in error, but he will build on the response and make clear that even a "wrong" answer can be used to open doors which otherwise might remain closed. He will demonstrate by his actions that no one in the room need fear an error; that in truth we profit more through error than through right answers learned by rote. Above all, he attempts to break through the protective façade of silence, for in most instances there can be no active involvement unless students are prepared to risk an opinion.

How one breaks through the silence is the key to any successful teaching methodology. This is where the skillful teacher demonstrates his art. It is not that the inner-city student is unable to communicate. On the contrary, he can relate to his classmates exceedingly well. He can recount the plot of a movie or of a television drama with ease. When describing an exciting happening in the cafeteria or an incident after a football game, ideas are expressed with verve and clarity.

Yet when asked to consider the westward movement in American history and to describe the fears and reactions of the Mexican government when hundreds of Americans began settling in Texas in the 1830s, he can utter only the most perfunctory response. Somehow anything which is "bookish" becomes difficult and threatening. He needs to be *shown* that he knows something. The teacher cannot simply pass on to someone else. Here is the time for the probing question, the reduction of the complex idea to the more simple—and once a response to the simple idea is achieved to begin the process of building. And here it is well to remember that the line separating the probing question from the needling question is quite fine. The insensitive teacher may cross it without being aware of the damage it may cause.

The department head is primarily a classroom teacher insofar as his time is spent each day, although his teaching load is reduced by one or two classes, depending on the number of teachers in his department. This being the case, the department head has the usual tasks of teaching to perform: He must meet his classes each day, plan his lessons, keep the records required in all schools, prepare and give examinations, grade papers, and involve himself in the countless routine jobs encountered by classroom teachers everywhere.

In addition to his classroom duties, he is also responsible for providing instructional leadership to the teachers in his department. He may be instrumental in making curricular changes, such as introducing new courses and deleting or changing others. This is the case now more than in former years, for currently there is (to borrow the title of countless social-studies meetings and seminar themes) "ferment in the social studies." This means there are pressures for including new courses in the secondary social-studies curriculum: sociology, anthropology, psychology, history of non-Western peoples, contemporary affairs, greater emphasis on geography and economics. The department head is expected to be knowledgeable about this welter of academic demands and be able to work with his department in assigning priorities.

This need to assign priorities is often complicated by the personal preferences of particular teachers in the department. It is not unusual for a teacher of world history, for example, to have majored in modern European history while in college and to have him seek every opportunity to teach his first love—modern European history. Whenever the topic of needed additional courses is discussed, he quite naturally pushes for modern European history, while someone else promotes sociology and still another pushes for contemporary affairs.

There is a reason other than that of being academically well prepared which plays a part in a teacher's promoting a new course for himself, and this reason is usually left unstated. Ordinarily a new course is introduced as an elective, and electives, by definition, are not meant for all students. It follows, then, that prerequisites may be listed which have to be met by students in order to be able to elect the new course. Whatever the stated reason for wanting the new course, it is likely that a major consideration is the fact that the new class will be screened, and only the more able students will be encouraged to enter. In the inner-city high school, this is indeed a major consideration.

It is an irony of the profession that most teachers wish to spend their time with students who least need them. The reasons for this are many and quite well understood. But the fact remains that too many teachers shun those who most need their assistance.

This is attested to by the ever-increasing number of in-service teacher seminars and workshops organized to better acquaint teachers with some of the complexities of working in the schools of the inner city. How many teachers have been perplexed, disappointed, and perhaps angered by lack of attention and by pupil laughter in the "wrong" places? Inexperienced teachers are particularly at a loss to explain why a class reacts as it does to discussions in

American history or geography. This is especially the case in junior high-school classes which are in predominantly Negro schools.

It requires great understanding and much reflection for a teacher to begin to grasp the significance of some of the laughter which comes at the wrong place. If the class is studying pre-Civil War America or the Reconstruction period or America as the land of the open society, where only hard work and ability matter in "getting ahead," the uneasy snickering may well be a nervous reaction to ideas which the junior high-school pupil is unable to respond to in any other way.

He knows that it just isn't so, but he is unable to challenge openly the ideas being treated in class. The result: uneasy, nervous laughter. Unfortunately, the Negro youngster simply doesn't feel a part of the picture. He doesn't truly belong, and he knows it.

And if the class begins a unit on sub-Saharan Africa, the unknowing teacher will expect some sympathetic reactions from the Negro youngster in class. It doesn't for some, for just as the Negro pupil feels he has no roots in American history, he also has none in Africa. He does *not* identify with African cultures. In fact, he is rootless. He cannot and will not identify with Negro slavery. His textbooks virtually refuse to acknowledge his existence after 1872, when the "unfortunate" period of Reconstruction in the South officially ended. And he has been erroneously taught that there was nothing but primitive, savage tribes in the Africa from which his ancestors were forcibly removed. He can feel no pride in this. So he is rootless, uncomfortable, unable to find out just where he does belong. He responds by laughing nervously. Given these circumstances it is the best he can do.

Finally, a few words on some of the problems encountered by a new, inexperienced teacher. These usually fall into two categories: classroom management and assessment of methods of instruction.

The pitfalls of poor classroom management are so numerous that rarely can the inexperienced teacher avoid an occasional fall. The organization of routines should be given more attention than it receives in teacher-preparation classes. But, no matter how carefully the novice is instructed, it is likely that he will find that certain organizational routines which should work simply do not.

How should written assignments be collected? How and when should attendance be taken? Should some examinations be corrected in class? When materials have to be distributed, how can it be done to avoid disrupting the class? If a group of students is being sent to the library for special work, how best to get them on their way? Questions such as these frequently are important enough to make the difference between a successful first year and a first year filled with disaster. The essential factor in most such instances is to organize routines in a manner which assures that the class will not be "lost" while the routines are carried out. For example, many classes will not simply wait quietly "with nothing to do" while the teacher arranges for a small group to go to the library at the start of the period.

The two categories, management and assessment, are so closely related that it is not possible to clearly delineate one from the other. In reality, it is organization which makes possible the building of a climate in the room which allows for instruction and learning.

The new teacher usually has not reached the level of professional development which enables him to capitalize on the unforeseen, to shift gears when the time is right. His tendency is to carry through with his original planning, which of course is usually the thing to do. However, fear of departing from a plan is responsible for the loss of many of the golden moments of teaching, moments when the teacher and his class strike intellectual fire.

Most important of all is the obligation to teach in such a manner as to make students reach out, to extend their horizons. If the course content is organized and presented in a manner as to make the goals so far removed as to be unattainable, most students will not even make the effort. The reverse is also necessary to understand. If content is too simple, a lesson becomes a sterile exercise. In either case, the teacher has lost his class, an unfortunate occurrence in any school, but especially so if the school is within the inner city.

*   *   *

There are some teachers—I believe "a few" would be more accurate, but optimism dictates the more positive "some"—in every inner city who are very concerned with the alienation of many minority group children, particularly Negro children. These teachers are also convinced that lessons need not be sterile exercises. Our next two contributors exemplify such teachers. Both were first-year teachers with remarkable sensitivities. Yet their humane insights are ironic, as we shall note later.

Underestimation
of *"Culturally Deprived"* Youth
by DONNA SCHWAB

After seeing movies akin to *The Blackboard Jungle* and reading sensational articles in urban dailies, one must easily imagine that schools in the slum areas of our large cities—Chicago, Detroit, Los Angeles, New York—are in truth madhouses in which, daily, thousands of raving juvenile delinquents are locked, searched for weapons, and held down at the brink of riot for six hours or so while harried teachers do their best to shout a bit of English or math. One might also believe that teachers are as likely to be smacked down or knifed as respected. One may imagine jeering, rude, and dirty teenagers hanging out windows, laughing and leering at female teachers, throwing equipment, and tearing up books.

On the other hand, recent articles about "cultural deprivation" might prepare one to expect poorly dressed, skinny, and undernourished children, unable to think or speak effectively. Along with this mental picture comes pity and the notion that we must make exceptions for difficulties such a child might be having in learning. After all, he has a "destitute" background and environment, and his only hope is to leave his "unstable" family. One would expect little from and hope to impose few limits upon this type of child. What he needs is "sympathy" and a "good stable job."

Both commonly drawn pictures are not only fallacious but malicious. Until we can look objectively at the students in our so called "depressed areas," look at them without fear or disgust, pity or condescension, we will continue to lose thousands of highly capable and potentially productive citizens each year. Too often there is little more wrong with our nation's criminals and welfare cases than a society and social class system which has viewed them with contempt or condescension from the day they entered school in Harlem, Watts, Southside Chicago, or wherever.

As a young teacher taking my first assignment in the city, I had been saturated with just such misconceived ideas. It is fortunate that I received my assignment in August. Had there been more than a month of tales, warnings, and pleadings not to take the job, I would surely have succumbed to panic and refused the assignment. I knew that all my students were to be Negro, which meant they would all be big, strong, stupid, unruly, sexually aggressive, criminally inclined, and musically talented. Outwardly poohpoohing warnings of stabbing and rape, I bravely marched up to the school in early September with a sureness of purpose that could not be shaken—except by the sight of barred and broken windows and an empty purse carelessly thrown into the bushes next to the steps. I turned just as surely around, marched back to the parking lot, and found another new teacher whose arm I could hold as we entered "the jungle."

Entering the school that morning began the gradual and sometimes painful process of peeling away prejudgments. Unfortunately, too many teachers seem never to succeed in peeping around the blinders of misconception and stereotype. They act accordingly and create situations which eventually do resemble their expectations. I'm not certain what made me so ready to accept my students in spite of all I thought I knew about them. I suspect it has something to do with a combination of gullibility and short memory, which had always before been concerned with extremely negative assets.

Admittedly, I found truth in some of what I had heard. To say otherwise would be to label the world as psychotic and myself alone as sane. We all know the next step for folks who begin to so view the world. I must admit that in a city high school of 3,000 Negro students (and three or four Caucasians for integration's sake, I suppose), I found more musical and dramatic talent than I had seen in a state university of 25,000 in the whole four years I attended. The talent programs resembled Birdland in comparison with the pantomimes and silly dance routines that I remember as being the substance of such shows in my own suburban high school. Who knows what lies behind such reputedly "racial" phenomena? Perhaps when scholars and researchers unravel such mysteries as the "poverty syndrome" and the "racial I.Q.," we will have an answer.

I must admit that I taught under extremely adverse conditions—physically, that is. One of the most sacred rules of the school was "no food at class parties." Naturally I broke it and found out why it had been made. The roaches ate my Christmas cookies before I could get them out for the kids. We had, all told, four fires, two floods, and one rat. My room seemed to be under the most crucial part of the boiler system because, each time it got cold, we watched workmen climb ladders through a hole in the ceiling as opposed to learning about metaphors. Perhaps it was all contrived to make the days more challenging. Besides, the conversations above our heads always gave us a chuckle or two. "Form and content unfit for classroom use" would undoubtedly have been the school board's evaluation.

Speaking of the "racial I.Q.," I can't help but think that an inhumane testing situation affects it to some degree. What suburban parent would stand for the administration of those Iowa Tests in a crowded, hot, and stuffy study hall with bells, conversations in adjacent rooms, roaring traffic outside, and no rest stops because "They'll never come back"? There is undoubtedly something dreadfully inadequate about the physical conditions we offer for the education of "deprived children."

As a third hearsay fulfilled, I admit that many of the kids in depressed areas are poor. The first time I forgot this fact was the last. I suppose I was unconsciously trying to prove myself a member of the "in group" of the lower socioeconomic level when I told my twelfth-grade honors English class of the "poor" family I had lived with while doing student teaching in England. "They had to sleep four in a bed," I remember explaining. "The conditions were very bad." Later in the week I had a delegation halt me after school to warn me of the toes I had stepped upon. "You're pretty well liked around here, you know," they told me firmly, "but you won't be for long unless you stop looking down your nose at us." At first I couldn't imagine what they were talking about and felt simultaneously flattered and alarmed. They went on to explain that "a lot of us sleep six and seven in a bed, and it's nothing we can help." I timidly thanked them for pointing out my attitude, and we sat on the steps for an hour or so discussing the possibilities of true communication between different races and social classes. It was the best lesson any of us had all year. I was informed that my "middle-classness" stuck out all over me and that after the excitement of "slumming" wore off I would marry a rich lawyer and go back to the suburbs. I disagreed, but only time will tell whose predictions were rooted in wisdom.

I had heard that a city kid fights for his life in a seedy environment that constantly threatened him, morally and physically. Many things confirmed this notion in my mind before the year was over. George was one of those sullen and bitter-looking students that a braver teacher might easily have been led to poke. I avoided him until he came in after school one day to inform me that I was not to try to make him read any of "those bold books." "I've only ever read one of them things," he continued. "It was called *Steel Shivs*. I know all about them and you's better find out too if you want to get along around here." He turned on his heel and stalked out. I became green and determined to ask for a transfer. I had no idea that my relationship with George would thicken, but it did. The next communication I had from him was a series of love letters in his journal. "See me," I wrote sternly at the bottom of the page before returning the notebook to him. When he finally did "see me" I had no more idea of how to handle an amorous eighteen-year-old (all 6 feet 4 inches of him) than I knew how to change a flat tire. In a purely instinctive gesture, I pulled myself up to my full 5 feet 4 inches, looked him straight in the chest, and shoved *A Primer of Freudian Psychology* into his stomach. "Go find out why you write love letters to your teacher," I stuttered. He did. The book was finished by the following morning, and he brought it back to me with a passage underlined in the section entitled "compensation." "Read that," he commanded defiantly and stomped off. He had underlined the explanation that unmarried teachers often teach in compensation for not having a family, which would be ultimately more desirable to them. George went on to read several other volumes of Freud's writings during the semester. Needless to say, his amour faded. It is impossible for romantic feelings to survive such heartless objectivity. We became, rather, formal friends in an unspoken truce of wits. At one point I asked him why he had to act so outwardly cold and bitter when we both knew he wasn't really this way at all. "Well, miss," he began, boring into me with his frank black eyes, "I live in the city and people out there know only one thing about me. Nobody messes with me. I learned it the hard way, miss, and I have two knife scars in my back to prove it." Skepticism fades in the face of physical evidence. I began to see that living itself can be a constant source of challenge. Many of the fellows I taught were never more than a suggestion away from narcotics peddlers, numbers runners, prostitutes, and other urban temptations. Most of us are aware of this fact, but I was surprised to find such an intricate subcultural pattern formed by the urban underworld. Early in the year I was informed of my own ignorance by a student surprised that I had never heard of Jimmy Joy, known to all as the most successful procurer in the city. "You know," someone else offered in casual conversation, "the one with the red Hog convertible—the only one with six gray foxes." "Oh, yes, of course," I choked, having learned the usefulness of concealed shock. Only then did I begin to realize the competition we frumpy old teachers were up against. I was determined to buy a red car.

It had always before been difficult for me to understand how urban kids manage to become so frequently entangled with the police department. The law often seems just another obstacle to growing up in the city. Somehow muddles such as Leroy's never occurred where I grew up, yet we know that boys are forever pushing their luck with the law, regardless of environment. I refuse to shout police brutality or racial discrimination, but after viewing several fiascos like the following, I am convinced that we really should offer a course on "how to live with the law." Leroy's offense grew from a simple traffic violation to contempt of court and resisting an officer, which resulted in thirty days in jail. This caused him to miss his finals, fail a semester, and graduate late by the skin of his teeth. Even more tragic perhaps, his girl would later have nothing to do with him. It takes guts to grow up in the heart of the city.

Finally, I must admit that far too many of our "culturally deprived students" have a real deficit of cultural experience. A youth who has spent seventeen or eighteen years in an urban ghetto knows more than many of us do about life in its barest and most concentrated form. He or she knows well every corner of the city and has no illusions about vice and virtue therein. However, to take that young person out of his element is to cause him to flounder. The school, unfortunately, is out of his element in many cases. Marlene assured me that Chicago is a state. Rebecca asked if New Delhi is a continent or a country. At times the tragedy of poor education made me extremely angry. At other times I couldn't resist a smile. I will never forget the day one of my students asked if I could get him a nice shirt to wear to a job interview. I borrowed an oxford-cloth, button-down-collared shirt from a friend and brought it to school. Robert quite liked his own image in what he called a "college boy's shirt" and decided right then and there to become one. It was the same lack of worldliness and sophistication that led him to ask the bus driver on a trip to a small, outlying city, "Can you let me off at Mr. Hill's house?" Never imagining that the bus driver might not know Mr. Hill, Robert was lost for hours. When I returned from a Christmas vacation in Florida, the students looked silently in horror at my sunburn for several days before cautiously and sympathetically asking about "that disease." They had never encountered a sunburn before, except perhaps on one of those "don't be a paleface" billboards. My Future Nurses' Club took extreme delight in making Easter baskets for the hospital. I had been hesitant to suggest the activity as an insult to their maturity, but soon realized that most had never had such a "cultural experience" before. Too easily we forget that Girl Scouts and summer-camp activities are not cultural universals. Finally, I saw the genuine eagerness of our urban youth for new people, places, and things when I invited a French exchange student from one of the suburban high schools to visit with us for the day. My students nearly devoured the poor girl with questions—many about race relations and economic conditions in France. Most had never met a foreign student. One of the teachers, whose class she visited, had the wisdom to leave his class alone with her. We will never know what they discussed, but we are sure from her enthusiasm about our school that the communication experience was truly rewarding. It is unfortunate that the invitation she extended to one of our students to visit the suburban school was seen as "impractical" by the administration there.

The preceding conceptions, seemingly correctly held about education in depressed areas, are only a small percentage of the total. Many conceptions generally held are simply not true. I expected discipline problems and had none—after I ignored two cherry bombs in the waste-basket, calmly hauled one young man back into the class-room after he had jumped out of a second story window to retrieve a shoe, and let my biggest showoff teach class for two days—he performed admirably! Somehow I learned early that a threat without a twinkle in the eye is useless. Not one student could possibly imagine that I really in-tended to turn him upside down and crack his head on the floor, but such promises led to better relations and quicker settling down than any serious fit I could have thrown.

Our greatest war is with apathy, not unruliness. School has, for many students, always been a frustrating and de-featingly negative experience. The law keeps most of them from physically dropping out, but hoards of them do their dropping out mentally. There were many signs of it. It seems to me that a student who comes to class with his coat on would probably rather be on his way out than his way in. Wearing sunglasses or "shades" is another simple symptom of our students' retirement from the scene. Per-haps a teacher could better spend her energies discovering why the student finds her so dull than in fighting with him to remove the evidence. After the first and only time I physically removed a student's sunglasses in compliance with school policy, revealing a painfully swollen black eye, much to the class's amusement, I decided that I would have only two rules in my classroom—come and read. Most of the kids think better with a wad of gum in their mouths anyway, I finally conceded. It's the oral commu-nication that gets a bit garbled. They stopped bringing food when they realized that I would most likely pass most of it around or eat it myself.

I firmly deny, after only one year of teaching in a

"slum" school, that we are contending with mentally dull juvenile delinquents. I would sooner accept the label "misdirected genius" in many cases. I remember trying to explain some insipid romantic intricacy in a sophomore text by drawing stick figures on the board to represent the characters. "This is Frank, this is Susan," I explained. Drawing a line to represent the barrier between them, I asked what problem or conflict kept Frank from his girl. "Well, mam," piped up an unchallenged wit in the back row, "the biggest problem is that he ain't got no arms." A similar incident confirmed in my mind that our students must often consider *us* "culturally deprived" or at the least silly and absent minded. Talking one day of Robert Frost, I had hoped to inspire my creative writers with a strikingly colored photograph of the old poet's face. "Does that look like your grandpa?" I cozily asked one of the apparently less mature fellows in the class. "No, mam," he straightened up quickly to assert. "My grandfather's black." I began to wonder whoever underestimated these well-formed minds.

Many discipline problems in the classroom obviously stem from boredom. Thinking we are dealing with slow learners, we water down curriculum and try to feed our students the results. Most of them aren't interested. We hand out stories of animals and adventures in old houses when many are ready for sociology and psychology in its most adult forms. Unfortunately, reading maturity does not parallel social maturity, so they read about animals, hot rods, and haunted houses until the day they leave school. Most of what could be of true interest and value to these students has been long labeled unfit for classroom discussion. Leonard was one of my especially misdirected geniuses. I found this to be true after he spent a short period in jail for an intricately contrived robbery. I have no doubt that he masterminded the whole thing. Had we been more perceptive about his energies and abilities when he was in grade school, he might have applied them to some socially useful task. He was extremely interested in electricity, and, when he returned to school late in the semester, he turned in a term paper that he had written in jail about electricity. The sources were all in his head. I confirmed the truth of his statements. It was an excellent paper, and I had to take it to someone in the field for content analysis. He passed English, but it will probably never be an asset to him. His record now is more impressively weighted with criminal offenses than A's in English.

Often we picture urban teenagers as rude, crude, and insulting. I think this depends upon the response they receive to what are often completely innocent remarks. For example, one of my first days on the job, I was leaving the school for lunch and was met halfway down the walk by a young man who whistled sailor style, rolled his eyes down to my feet, and said, "I know you ain't no teacher." "Why?" I asked, rather curiously. "Because you got too big legs!" he expressed with obvious sincerity. I laughed it off nervously and went on wondering just how deeply I had been insulted. I later found that it was apparently a complimentary remark and was relieved that I hadn't tried to pull him by the ear to the office. He would probably have knocked me out with one swift blow. Anyway, he showed up later in the English office to carry books and equipment around for me. I guess he just wanted to look at my legs because he never talked much. One night, I went to a P.T.A. meeting not realizing it would be dark when I returned home. As comfortable as I had come to feel inside the school, it still made me squeamish to wait on the corner for a bus, and I really had no desire to do so in the dark. I grabbed one of my students (often considered to be quite a threat to women himself) and asked him for his protection while I waited for the bus. He was unduly charmed and lectured me for ten minutes about the necessity for being very careful by myself at night. I suppose it is difficult for any man to refuse an invitation to play the knight. I found that too frequently, female-dominated young men are only too eager to play their rightful roles as gentlemen.

Perhaps even too eagerly so. One day a few of my boys came to me with a surprise. They wanted to "help me out." I was delighted until I found they had stolen four whitewall tires for my car. They had been feeling sorry that my car was the only one in the parking lot with black tires. Loyalty among thieves, or something like that, I suppose. Apparently this kind of activity had no taboo at all within their value system. All property is communal, but one must never steal from his friends, according to a well-defined subculture. It was indeed a predicament! I made up an incoherent story about some whitewalls in storage for summer someplace and asked them to *please* return the tires to their owner. They did, fortunately with no complications. What particularly interested me was that none of them had any apparent interest in looting for its own sake. They had sincerely hoped to help a lady out! A favor once rejected is never offered again, thank goodness!

I was told when I took the job that I would have to handle many kids who made their way in the world by telling stories. Unfortunately, I went on this assumption for a while until I had thoroughly embarrassed myself by believing the worst and then having to apologize. Our first trip to the public library was enough to cure me of any remaining skepticism. Fifteen minutes after we arrived, Oscar approached me to say he was leaving to babysit for his mother while she went to the hospital to have a baby. "Sure, you are," I said and smugly hauled him off to the telephone in order to publicly expose his unlikely story. Mrs. Jones was obviously awaiting his arrival. She was about to have her seventh child. I congratulated her and apologized, feeling extremely silly. A few hours later I had the library guards searching the grounds for two of my problem cases. I was sure they had taken a permanent break to visit a nearby poolhall or something. After causing a public spectacle, we found them down in the vaults, earnestly taking notes out of some ancient jazz magazines. They hadn't realized you could *read* about such things. I soon learned to keep my big mouth shut.

What is probably the most tragic misconception we have about educating the "culturally deprived" child is that notion that we must change our curriculum to meet his low academic abilities. It is commonly assumed that we cannot teach *these* students the classics. Fiddlesticks! We can teach them anything under the sun if it is presented in the right way. The point should be rather that the classics are often a waste of time for a student who will never have more than a high-school education. When he is crying out for information about his own world, about himself as part of a race, part of a generation of men and women. The students who took part in "freedom school," during a recent high-school boycott in Detroit, expressed a desire to know about laws affecting their rights as citizens, about their own history as a race in America, about their own minds' and bodies' workings. They wanted to talk about religion, Africa, and segregation in the South.

It was obvious to all those who listened to them that public schools are doing very little to help the urban Negro youth answer his one burning question: "Who am I?" Some classics can help him. I taught Shakespeare's *Othello* and Steinbeck's *Of Mice and Men* with encouraging results because we discussed the people as real and the social and moral question in familiar terms. My greatest delight came when the argument over Othello's sanity got to such a pitch that one of my "juvenile delinquents" stood up and shouted: "You put your money where your mouth is, man. That cat's mind's messed up!" Only curiosity about my laughter stopped a full-scale battle. They never did figure out why I thought it was so funny. On the other hand, "A Child's Christmas in Wales" was an absolute bore to the entire class because of its fantasy-like situations, which I hadn't prepared to translate into anything pertinent to their lives.

I've decided that nothing is really beyond the capabilities of these "deprived" students if they are well prepared for an experience. My twelfth graders chose to attend two plays at the nearby university as a substitute for purchasing a grammar book. (They weren't actually getting away with as much as they thought they were, however, since I had already decided which experience would be the most educational.) They buzzed over *The Tempest* and *She Stoops to Conquer* like seasoned old theatergoers, even though only a handful had ever attended a play before. They immediately sympathized with Ariel and Caliban, and the bawdy humor in *She Stoops* was all very clearly appreciated (interestingly so, in view of what we so often believe about "dialect barriers"). I did have one particularly miserable failure as a "bearer of culture" to my students. It was the evening I took a young man to hear the local symphony.

He was so full of nothing that I had hoped to spark him to the world of values with some good music. For the duration of the concert he counted fur coats, putting them in categories of "dog hair" and "bearskin." I was crushed, until he told me he couldn't dig that kind of stuff because it didn't have any . . . "you know . . ." and he pounded out a complicated syncopated rhythm on the dashboard of the car. "Beat," I added, defeated but fully appreciating the point!

Finally, my first year of teaching in the city proved to me that these students do not need sympathy. They don't want it and furthermore reject anyone soft enough to grant the compensations they ask. Any teacher gullible enough to fall for the inevitable story, "my little sister ate my homework," without demanding a new version of the same, deserves the reputation she will soon have to live with. Winning sympathy becomes a full-time occupation for many students who have never had to lift a finger to pass a class. The evils of social promotion are well documented by reports of failures of Negro students as college freshmen. Sympathy and double standards are the cruelest gifts we can confer upon our "culturally different" students. It is something I learned the difficult way.

Joseph was not in my classes, but he knew I liked him and brought me poetry to read. He also knew I would loan him money and help him out of messes he got himself into. I was taken, I suppose, by his "artistic sensitivity" and allowed him to squirm out of many situations that should have been faced up to. He told me in many ways to set limits for him, but I didn't. He showed his disapproval by destroying a portable radio I had allowed him to borrow and take home. Joseph is, I realize now, only one representative of many students who resent overindulgence and the lack of standards demanded of them by people looking with sympathy. They plead for respect and a sense of importance. Joseph was finally expelled from school for wearing a "Malcolm X" button around in the halls. Unfortunately, in his search for respected identity, he had seized upon the undeniably charismatic figure of Malcolm X. No one allowed him to mention or question this new-found interest, so he went off defeated and humiliated. For one emotionally unstable youngster, he certainly upset one large professional faculty. Fortunately, kids are unbelievably flexible, and he returned to school dragging all of Dick Gregory's books and records. Apparently this threatened no one's sense of decorum, and he was allowed to remain.

Many articles have been written about the failure of our public schools to deal with students of other-than-white, middle-class upbringing. Few explain just how tragically we really are failing to help them grow. It is hoped that some of the preceding anecdotes will tell the story better than tables and statistics. Our schools are full of dissatisfied youth and wasted potentials. The first move we must make as citizens and educators is to clear away our misconceptions and face the problem as it is, making use of the positive factors and working to reduce the negatives.

Teach Them Passivity
by MIRIAM DANN

The recent student walkout at —— High School pointed out one unquestionable fact: Negro youth is not being educated. If you doubt this, you have never seen Detroit's schools. What are they like? As a teacher in one of Detroit's inner-city schools not far from ——, I present the following description of my high school:

Population: nearly 3,000
Time: 1966
Atmosphere: one of suspicion and hostility, a dictatorship in miniature, where all basic freedoms (of speech, of the press, and so forth) are denied.

A student sits staring out of the classroom window. He is bored with the work. He studied all this in the sixth grade down South. Now, in the twelfth grade, he is thinking of dropping out. Nobody cares about him. He sees his counselor only when a school official finds him doing something wrong.

A tenth-grade student stumbles into the classroom. His records show that since the second grade his teachers have been recommending psychiatric help. Nothing has been done. He wanders from class to class without books or supplies because he will not bring them. He stares blankly at the walls around him until some teacher gets fed up with him and he is suspended for a few days, after which time he returns, only to be suspended again.

What happens to students who feel hostility toward the school and the teachers, who feel discouraged, unchallenged, and unwanted? Does the school attempt to overcome his fears? No. The officials wait until he shows his anger, and then he is suspended.

Is there any help for the many students who have psychological problems or who come from homes where they have been beaten into submission or futile rebellion? No. They are taught to have an unquestioning acceptance of whatever their "superiors" tell them. They must never rebel, never express their own opinions, and must suppress in school everything that is not "nice" or "middle class." If they refuse to accept a position of inferiority, they soon learn that the school does not want them.

In such an authoritarian atmosphere, it is no wonder that students have trouble learning. When a teacher comes into the school system, he is told that he must always be a model of middle-class morality. He must always stifle anything which is "Negro" or "lower class" in the students. For example, when I want to discuss literature that deals with the environment of the students, I am told that "this is highly inappropriate because the students might think that the language and people in the stories are 'all right'." This is consistent with the school policy, which wants to teach them to reject their environment.

If the school teaches the student to be ashamed of his environment, his language, and his hope, this is tantamount to teaching the student to hate himself. If the school does nothing to make the student feel more acceptable than he feels at home and in society, then it loses its ability to educate. For a student must have some faith in himself and his ability before he will learn. A boy who is sure he can never make a basket will not try out for the basketball team. A student who is convinced that he is inferior is in the same position.

What are the results of an atmosphere in which the teachers are actively discouraged from being open and friendly to the students and few, if any, people have any faith in their ability to learn? The result is that, as in my school, the average reading level of the students is sixth grade, which means that many are reading at a third-, fourth-, and fifth-grade level. The school has set up no standards which the students must pass before passing from one grade to another. The textbooks are so boring and unimaginative that the average teacher finds her efforts to stimulate the students almost defeated before she begins. There is almost no time for individual instruction. The average teacher has between 150 to 170 students a day, with only thirty-five minutes to check papers, settle individual matters, and contend with such things as attendance and other administrative matters.

Most classrooms have between thirty and thirty-six students in them. The students in the back often cannot see the teacher. Sometimes they fall asleep, indifferent and unnoticed. The school is old and dirty. Roaches crawl freely around the lunchroom, and mice slither across the rooms. The paint is peeling in the classrooms, and when it rains the ceilings leak.

Any criticism of the school is taken by the officials as a personal insult. So, while every single student in my school could be achieving at a much higher level with the proper instruction, changes in classroom procedure are negligible. Requests that more kindness and understanding be used in dealing with the students are usually met with the answer, "They don't respond to that kind of treatment."

The thing that disgusts me most about the school system is the attitude toward the students. It could be summed up by a remark which two Negro teachers made to me after the —— incident: "I think we teachers should walk out and protest inferior students."

When I signed my teacher's contract with the Detroit Board of Education, I did not think to demand certain rights which should be inherent in any school system: the right to treat students with respect and give them the freedom to think for themselves. I should have demanded the right to refuse to insult their intelligences by spoon feeding them hypocritical untruths of white authors or "acceptable" Uncle Toms like Booker T. Washington. I should have demanded the right to refuse to go along with administrative policies which shamed and humiliated students in a hundred little ways—for wearing a hat in school, for being in the halls without a pass, for not being able to read. It seems to me to be the duty of a teacher to teach her students to be intellectually honest, to criticize and question everything and anything without fear of reprisal, and most of all to be proud of themselves and their culture, so that the endless centuries of discrimination and injustice against them might somehow be brought to an end through the end of their self-hatred.

I didn't demand those rights. I entered the school system and just quietly refused to do those things which were against my principles. If I felt like having lunch with a student, driving a student home after school to meet his parents or discuss something that was bothering him, or discussing police brutality and prejudice with a group of students during my lunch hour, I simply did those things. If classroom material was boring and childish, I brought in literature which challenged their minds and matched their degree of social sophistication, which is far above that of the average middle-class child. Recognizing their lack of pride in themselves and their Negro heritage, I exposed them to the tremendous accomplishments of Africans and American Negroes. With curiosity and confusion, they read the poetry of authors like Claude McKay, who wrote:

> If we must die—let it not be like hogs
> Hunted and penned in an inglorious spot,
> While round us bark the mad and hungry dogs,
> Making their mock at our accursed lot.
> If we must die—oh, let us nobly die,
> So that our precious blood may not be shed
> In vain; then even the monsters we defy
> Shall be constrained to honor us though dead!
> Oh, Kinsmen! We must meet the common foe;
> Though far outnumbered, let us show us brave,
> And for their thousand blows deal one deathblow!
> What though before us lies the open grave?
> Like men we'll face the murderous, cowardly pack,
> Pressed to the wall, dying, but fighting back!
>
> (Claude McKay, "If We Must Die," in *Se-lected Poems of Claude McKay*. Reprinted by permission of Twayne Publishers, Inc.

Most of my students had been taught for so long to turn the other cheek and never fight back against anybody except people of their own color that at first they could not understand the philosophy of "Negro protest." But it was not long before they, themselves, were writing poetry of militant protest and bitter denunciations of Negro oppression. It was not long before I began to hear students in the halls discuss the accomplishments of Negro writers

and inventors and scientists so that students of other
teachers asked me for the poems and came to sit in on my
classes.

It was also not long before complaints began to come
to me from other teachers and administrators. They accused me of teaching the students to disrespect authority
and question what was being taught and "planting the
seeds of violence in their minds," as the gym teacher said.
My department head accused me of "teaching these students to hate white supremacy and Uncle Toms." Finally,
the other teachers said I was teaching rebellion and hate.
Hate? If an American Negro does not feel any hostility
toward what white people have done in this country, then
he must be deaf, dumb, blind, and mentally ill. After 400
years of oppression, which has mocked every code of civil-
ization and humanity ever set forth, how can Negroes,
young or old, fail to be indignant? And as for rebellion?
Well, when have you ever respected someone you could
step on? I wasn't teaching rebellion, I was merely letting
my students know that it was all right to refuse to be de-
graded and deprived and exploited. They feel that way
inside. *They know* they're not getting a fair deal in this
country. Should we teach them that what they know and
feel is wrong? The average Negro student who comes from
a poverty-ridden area *is already bitter and angry inside*.
What I want to teach them is not to turn that anger and
bitterness against themselves in self-destructive acts, but to
turn it against those people and institutions which made
them that way, which forced them to feel the sense of
worthless and hopelessness which keeps them from getting
an education and perpetuates the system of exploitation
and the cycle of inescapable poverty.

One of the most perceptive critics of the system was

Malcolm X. When I brought his record *Message to the Grass Roots* into the classroom, the students were thrilled and excited to an extent I had never seen before. He put into words something that almost all of them felt inside but were afraid to acknowledge: that something is rotten in the United States—a truth that most Negroes in America will learn to stifle and deny by the time they are out of their teens. Malcolm spoke to them. He spoke their language. He spoke to the boys who will soon be going to die in Vietnam while they are denied the right to fight for their own people. He spoke to those students who go out with only lighter skinned dates because they feel that the latter are somehow "better." And he made that one statement which so few are willing to see is true: that in the past 400 years, nothing has been gained by Negroes who were passive and who refused to rebel against the system.

In an effort to compensate for some of the tremendous deficiencies of the school system, I tried to institute new programs from the time I started teaching. For example, I wrote a special grammar book for my students using their language, songs, and slang, and which they enjoyed more than the usual type of grammar book which constantly told them they were "wrong." I also developed a program designed to give all students with reading problems a double period of English, using very small classes and understanding, sympathetic teachers, who would take a personal interest in the students and thereby help to motivate them to do better in their studies. Along with other teachers from the school system, I was chosen last year by the board of education to write a Negro literature unit for use in all high schools. After completing the work, however, my department head told me that it would not be used at our high school because he felt white students needed it more than ours did!

Despite all my efforts to help the students, I was informed last March that I was being transferred from the school. One official paper said, "she seems to take too much interest in the students and the community." I was terribly dismayed; not for myself, but for my students, many of whom felt that school was a cold and hostile place, except for the presence of a few concerned teachers, who always seemed to be transferred soon after they came to the school.

What they need is an atmosphere of flexible discipline, warmth, and understanding. This is what I tried to achieve in my classroom. However, my success with the students only seemed to increase the ire of my associates and "superiors." The only hope for the future lies in the increased awareness of young people about what is being done to them and the concerted efforts of community leaders, as well as the youth, to *militantly* fight the inequities that have been kept hidden from the public via meaningless diplomas and endless promises from hypocritical public officials.

Let us remember what Frederick Douglass once said: "Power concedes nothing without a demand." If we know who is the "power" in this society, then we will know who is keeping our children shackled and enslaved in submission, fear, and ignorance.

* * *

The irony of these two selections is implicit in the latter article. Both authors are young women who started their teaching careers at the same high school, and both left the profession after one year. Both admit that they have much to learn about teaching, but who doesn't. In any case, their values and goals appear to be exactly those that we claim are needed in urban teachers. Yet they did not make it. Rather than be transferred to another school, one resigned. The other took a leave of absence. Both began advanced studies at nearby universities, their interest in teaching, in urban problems, and in kids still high, but their view of school systems and of some teachers and administrators understandably somewhat negative. Such teachers are all too rare in the schools, and their departure is thus a serious loss. They represent the kind of people who should be encouraged in every way possible to remain in teaching. Happily, one of the authors has accepted another teaching position. We can only suggest that most school systems put a premium on creativity, as long as that creativity is *not* related to controversial issues. Working closely with older Negro students and encouraging them to question the ways of our society (including that of our schools) is one of the taboo areas in education. These attitudes would threaten the system even if the students were white, though, in this era of civil-rights controversies, anything to do with Negro youth becomes much more "dangerous."

We are not judging the details of either of our contributors' experiences as first-year teachers. We are strongly suggesting, however, that any teacher who begins to encourage students to question their society is in for a rough time. Only a minority of educators (teachers, principals, and college professors) would encourage such young teachers to remain in the profession and to fight it out. Not that most teachers, principals, and college professors are not decent folk. But perhaps the problem is that so many educators are good, "decent" Americans who simply want to avoid some of the more ugly facets of our way of life. Like so many other Americans, educators are not likely to become actively involved in the "good fight." One could wish that more of them were supportive and accepting of the kind of activities that our last two contributors represent. We can only suggest that the activist is not likely to be attracted to teaching; and, when he is, he is likely to get his lumps. This may not sound very enticing, but "that's the way it is, baby."

But there *are* educators who welcome such teachers, and that is most encouraging. These teachers can make it but only if they are placed in the right schools, where the key administrators are also beyond the lip-service stage. There are such people in every school system, but their number is not large. Perhaps it is increasing, but the probability that activists will be welcomed into the teaching profession is still overwhelmingly negative.

Our final contribution is from a principal who gives an overview of his responsibilities. His observations introduce still other aspects of life in an urban school. The tenor of his remarks suggests that perhaps our two "rebels" might still be in the classroom had they been assigned to his school. But this is merely conjecture. There is nothing theoretical in his writing, however. It clearly states some of the concerns faced daily by any competent principal.

Some Thoughts
on a Principalship
by FREEMAN FLYNN

One cannot discuss the role of the principal in the inner
city or so-called inner-city school without first defining
some terms. There are many inner-city schools; there are
many principalships, depending upon the size of the school
and the character of the community. Every school district
has a distinct flavor of its own. One might not be aware
of this by driving down the streets; one poor community
looks like any other poor community. The fact is, the history of a particular area within the inner city determines
to a large extent the mood, the tone, the understanding
of the community, and the relationship of a community
to its school. In addition, the size of the school, the number of children who attend the school, the staff and personnel policies which have affected that particular school
all have to be considered in determining the efficiency,
the communication between the school and its community, and many other factors. The principal in this situation sometimes finds that he will have other principals
who are dealing with problems similar to his and who
understand his problems. It is also possible that he really
is quite alone and that there are few people who really

understand him and the problems he is dealing with. Further, it is very possible that his staff may not see his job and his responsibilities in the same light that he does. That is, an individual school has to be examined carefully, and the individuals working within the school have to examine themselves in relation to their job.

Let me illustrate the preceding by telling something of my own community. The school in which I work has approximately 1,850 children, 82 professional staff members, and 37 clerks, cleaning people, engineers, janitors, and lunchroom people. Recently a Federal program has added a total of 47 teacher and staff aides, supervised by the principal. Of the professional staff members, at present thirty-seven of the eighty-two are people who have finished less than two years of teaching. Another five have less than two years of experience in Detroit. Obviously, we are talking about a staff of beginners, many of whom are in the process of learning to do their job while doing it.

The community in which the school is located is unique and has undergone many severe problems. Following World War II an examination of this community would have disclosed a middle-class, mainly Jewish structure fringed by an area of very wealthy homes. This community went through a very rapid change: The middle-class community moved out and was supplanted by an upper lower-class Negro community. The period of transition took place in about seven or eight years. From 1950 to 1957–1958, the school-student population changed from somewhere in the neighborhood of 15 per cent Negro children to 95 per cent Negro children. The school population merely reflected what was happening in the total community surrounding the school. Following this very drastic social revolution, a second revolution began almost at once. The urban renewal crisis of the city tended to clear out large amounts of downtown slum areas, and the people were lifted bodily and transported out of those areas. They tended to come into the areas such as this one in large numbers. Illustrative of this, one of the elementary schools in the community had a rise in its student population in the past five years from approximately 1,400 to 2,400 children. The newcomers to the community came from the bottom of the social scale, crowding in on a group who had achieved middle-class status and who considered themselves upwardly mobile.

As this social change took place, the staff, which had been in the early 1950s largely an older and mature group with long experience in the schools, found that the problems in the school were increasingly difficult to handle. They became increasingly discouraged and dismayed by their inability to relate to problems crowding in upon them in their school and were increasingly at a disadvantage in dealing with children whose performance in school was different from that which they had been accustomed to. As a result, the turnover in the staff increased, and the reputation of the school suffered in the professional community and in the eyes of the parents. In recent years, as integration and civil rights became a crusading force, the school system responded by opening up many schools on a so-called open school basis and permitted parents to transfer their children into those schools freely, as the parents were willing to pay for the transportation. This tended to accentuate a factor which had been occurring, that is, the middle-class Negro parents either packed up and moved again into a community which, in turn, was repeating the experience that our community had already experienced; or, finding it difficult to find another place to live, took advantage of the open-school policy and took the child out of the school, thus removing from the school those children most able to do traditional school work and most able to cope with traditional school demands. Performance levels of classes went down and down; test scores for the schools revealed a decreasing achievement level. The teacher's satisfaction in dealing with children became increasingly frustrated and confused. The new teacher especially found it difficult to break into such a school, and the staffing policies of the board of education were affected because the school tended to be recognized as a difficult place to teach. The board began assigning men to the building until the number of men in the school was well beyond two-thirds of the total staff. This tended to create a masculine air in the junior high school. Children had come to the school from the basically matriarchical society of the community and the matriarchical pattern of the elementary school.

The masculinity tended to be reflected in strong measures for discipline, such as increasing evidence of the use of the paddle. There were many indications that the school was not responding in a satisfactory way to the conditions presented to it, but rather responding and reacting in anger and desperation. Frustrated, teachers tended to look around for someone to blame, and the principal happened to be a very convenient scapegoat. The teacher's organization tended to look upon the principal in such a school as being one who was responsible for maintaining discipline; and, if the dimensions of the job were impossible, that still didn't change the understanding of the principal's role by the teaching group. In some schools with similar problems, principals were able to create a relatively stable situation through strong loyalties on the part of those staff members who were more able to understand what was the situation in the school.

The differences in the understanding on the part of the teachers are also, however, a reflection of the differences in the communities. For instance, some schools have been in the midst of slum areas a long time. They have succeeded in establishing a kind of school behavior that contrasts with home behavior, and children tend to become schizophrenic, if you will, with two standards of behavior: one for school and one for home. This can be seen and demonstrated in school after school at the elementary level and, in particular, with the one Negro high school that existed for many years in the city. Following World War II, however, as the Negro population increased in the city and the number of schools that changed from white to Negro increased, the problems became more and more glaringly apparent. Again, the elementary school, probably because of its smaller size, the age of its children, and perhaps because of the "softening" influence of the women who composed the majority of the faculty, did not present the same challenges that the junior high—and at times the senior high schools—have presented over the last ten years or so. It is perfectly apparent, if one steps back and examines the problems that arose in such schools, that the problems were greater than the collective ability of the staff members. As a result, school after school developed morale problems, and teachers left the inner city with bitter feelings. At the same time, many teachers found tremendous satisfaction in their jobs and found that they could have very successful experiences in their classroom. This did not mean, however, that they invariably found that they maintained a successful professional relationship with all of their colleagues.

To some extent, we can sum it up by saying that there were those who could and those who couldn't, and, of all the staff and the members of the community, the principal was obviously the man in the hot seat. His role in public relations is critical and very difficult. In a highly transient community, finding the individuals who can lend strength to parent groups, finding the individuals who will support the schools, and finding the people who understand what the schools are trying to do is not an easy task. The problems that confront the principal daily in such schools are not really different from the problems that confront principals in any public school. It seems to me, however, that such problems are more numerous, more demanding, and come at the principal with a fashion and a violence which makes reasonable solutions extremely difficult. It is not unusual for a principal to have to deal with a series of problems like the following, in the course of an ordinary morning's work.

For instance, the principal may come into school and find waiting for him an angry parent who is concerned about the fact that a teacher has slapped her child the day before. The principal must work on the problem cold as he starts his day. The techniques of handling angry parents are, of course, known to all principals in the business. This is part of the trade, but to start the day like this is like walking into a cold shower without any preparation. Following such an incident, one might easily find himself involved with a dispute, for instance, between two teachers. There is often a question between teachers as to whether equity exists in assignments. While trying to referee such a problem, the principal may also have to attend to a child who has been injured in a fight. One might, in conference with social workers and other individuals working with a particular child, have the conference interrupted by a false fire alarm from one of the eighteen stations that exist in the building. Any of the above problems could happen even before the school day begins. Because of a shortage of substitutes, the assistant principal might wish to consult as to how the school will operate with a staff one to four teachers short.

Fortunately, today, possible solutions to some of the troubles outlined in the foregoing are beginning to appear. Federal money, mentioned earlier, is providing teacher aides (who have to be trained); supplementary funds (which have to be spent by committees representing staff, children, and community); special programs for student employment; in-service workshops for upgrading the professional staff; and other developments to aid in improving the school. It is obvious that care in planning for the utilization of such assistance is a part of the principal's role. Much of it has to be done at home, in order to gain necessary time to think through the various aspects of each. Consultation with people within the building and from central staff is a necessary part of each new program. Evaluation and supervision of all parts of the school operation require managerial skills that increasingly call for familiarity with a wide range of educational matters. And last, the role of leader requires that the principal be immediately accessible to students, to teachers, to noncontract employees, and to parents.

Again, it seems to me that all of the foregoing is common to principals everywhere. The differences between one school and another, however, are great, and the sheer volume of demand for the principal's time, attention, and energy varies considerably. At the same time, the principalship of a large inner-city junior high school provides a

continuous participation as a central figure in a dynamic
process. The public schools of America are in the process
of change, largely forced upon them by circumstances and
as a by-product of the civil-rights drama. In short, they
are "where the action is," and, if one is alive, that is where
one wants to be!

*   *   *

We see no need to underscore or review the message
of this last contribution or of any of the others. Each of
our contributors has spoken for himself, and we leave it
to the reader to accept or reject the views presented.
For our part, we accept and support the theme of each
selection and see no need to debate minor points here
or there. Although our several spokesmen do not cover
the total spectrum of issues and problems in urban
schools, they represent the thoughtful and insightful
teacher and administrator who are so badly needed in
many schools. They all imply that only a teacher or administrator who cares about students, who has the
strength to put up with or to challenge some of his
peers, and who knows the system well will make an impact in an urban school. He will be working with some
people who work hard and may be trying to seek better
ways; he will also be working with some who are simply
putting in their time.

As long as a principal or teacher is willing to examine
all of the premises of the system and his role in it, there
is hope. There is also more than hope. There is the fact
that any large urban school contains a few people who
are dedicated to being "where the action is." It is from
this minority that both inspiration and support can be

drawn. If the neophyte teacher learns who these people are, he may well become one of the contributors to progress in his school. It is also possible he may have to be the first one in his building to begin asking the kinds of questions that challenge the *status quo*. Whatever the situation, he must be prepared for negative reactions as well as support. If he is not aware of the turmoil in values and the range of problems permeating every urban school, it is quite likely that he will join the ranks of the docile majority. We already have enough of these teachers. The real need is for more people who are prepared to examine what they and the schools are doing both *for* and *to* children—a subtle distinction, perhaps, but one of fundamental import.

Chapter 5

The
Community
Study

Implicit throughout our discussion is the principle that the teacher must be a student of the social system of the school. The new teacher must be especially sensitive to the nature of the system if he is to resist the pressures that contribute to a pattern of conformity and rigidity. He needs to appraise the traditional responsibilities placed on him, the chains of command within the system, both the formal and informal rules and regulations binding on teachers and students, and the social pressures that face him. Normative positions often preclude rational examinations of practices. For example, there is the perhaps apocryphal tale of one school staff that persisted in not permitting students to use the front door to the building and resisted questions from its principal about the reason for this rule. The only answer given was that it had "always" been the rule. The original reasons for the prohibition were lost in antiquity, yet generations of students were enjoined to keep away from the front door for no meaningful purpose. A more telling rationale for a critical appraisal of school practices is inherent in an examination of the urban teacher's relationship to the neighborhood in which he is teaching. For generations, the literature of education has expounded the idea that the effective teacher must know all he can about the backgrounds and community of his children. This theme has been reemphasized in recent years as concern about the disadvantaged has increased. We have already suggested some of the definitions of the inner city currently in use, and it is clear that much research remains to be done. Some of this research can be done by the classroom teacher.

Research may be undertaken at various levels. There is no question that the majority of graduates from teacher-training institutions have had little encouragement to examine systematically the various dimensions of their work. That a research orientation is vital in the development of a well-trained teacher is not a common premise among all teacher educators, however. In fact, some university professors resist involving undergraduates in research activities on the grounds that they lack sufficient maturity, background, or training. We shall justify the need for a research orientation by arguing that teachers who are not willing to examine teaching practices and their own behavior as objectively as possible have little chance of ever becoming true professionals. They may well be able to perform the various routines associated with teaching at an instinctive level.

But there is more to teaching than one's *feelings* about children or the school. One's personal satisfactions are but one index of creative teaching. There is also a need for a research-oriented perceptiveness.

The lack of a research orientation among many teachers is neatly demonstrated by the rather profound ignorance of many, many urban teachers about the areas in which they teach. It has been suggested by more than one wag that the typical inner-city school is somewhat like a medieval castle. That is, it is a fortress that opens to the serfs in the area early in the day; the staff of the castle then draws the drawbridge until the end of the school day; the bridge is later lowered with the inevitable rush for home, with some of the teachers beating the pupils on the way out. To put it another way, most urban teachers live nowhere near the schools to which they are assigned. Most of these teachers simply drive in and out of the school area and have very little intimate knowledge of living conditions, aspirations, problems, joys, or, to put it very simply, life in the area.

This charge is hotly debated by some teachers. They argue that they have been teaching in a given school for five or ten years, so they know the area; that during that time they have worked with hundreds, if not thousands, of children; that there have been all kinds of open-house parties and parental conferences at which they have met with some of the parents; that many of the children tell them of incidents in the neighborhood and in the home; that some of the old-timers have indeed had three or four children from the same family and are thus "very closely" acquainted with that family. All these arguments are valid, and certainly these experiences can help any perceptive teacher learn about life in the neighborhood. The majority of even well-meaning teachers, who feel that they are informed about the community in which they teach, are likely to have only superficial insights into the area, however. Many are only "experts through the classroom window." Or, to expand the concept, some of them are "experts through the car window." They do see some aspects of the community through these windows, for example, some of the housing conditions. But the greater part of these teachers never attempt to make conscious, planned, and systematic appraisals of life in the area. Fewer still wish to become identified with the neighborhood; not necessarily as residents, but as people who feel free to visit homes, to shop in the area, to attend community meetings, or to walk its streets. The need for teachers to see their charges in other than a student role is self-evident, if one is committed to the "whole child" concept. The behavior of a child in his peer-familial-community life space is frequently different from the behavior demonstrated in the classroom.

Some teachers are incapable of becoming students of the school's area. Others simply refute any suggestion that they learn about the area, for this idea is contrary to their view of a teacher's role. These types of teachers believe that the school exists only to teach children and not to serve as a social agency. They argue that it is the job of the social worker to work with the parents at home. Still other teachers have entered the profession as a retreat from life, and this group certainly cannot be counted on in any school-community "get acquainted" activities. Even teachers who see the value of learning more about the community often fear the area in which they work, particularly if they are white teachers working in Negro neighborhoods and vice versa.

Most teacher-training programs designed to prepare better urban teachers are beginning to confront these attitudes and fears. They strongly urge their students to become involved in community studies. In the Teacher Corps, for example, the preservice portions of the program focus on the variety of ways that the interns can learn about the life styles of the areas in which they will be working. These activities may include living in the area for a period of time, walking tours of the area, conducting interviews, visiting agencies, examining census materials, getting acquainted with indigenous leaders, visiting homes, and so on. The essential goal of such activities is, not only to provide the prospective teacher with insights and information about the inner city or poorer sections of the city, but also to encourage the neophyte to examine his personal value structure in relation to what he sees and hears. Although a portion of our new generation of teachers is participating in such activities and self-examinations in their training, many other neophyte teachers are not. Furthermore, the teaching staffs of urban schools are made up of tens of thousands of teachers who were trained twenty and thirty years ago and have never been challenged to study their communities. In the previous chapter, we stressed that the teacher's positive attitude toward students is a key to better teaching in urban schools. Developing positive attitudes toward clients is one aspect of training in any profession. The fact that teacher training does not always attain this goal is reflected in other professions. We know that this is the case from the reports of those educators who are seeking to implement new programs, curricula, and opportunities for disadvantaged youth. Over and over we hear that, unless teachers respect their students, most of the money and effort expended to improve education will be ineffective—though some children may be reached in some ways. Respect is not likely to develop, however, unless urban teachers learn the ways of life in their schools' neighborhoods and reflect their knowledge in school activities. Development of respect is too important to be left to chance in both pre-service and in-service training.

Let us become more specific. We believe that any teacher worth his salt in an urban school, or in any school for that matter, must do his best to learn about his school's community. Without knowledge of the community, it is unlikely that the teacher's day-by-day work with his students will be relevant to their life styles and aspirations. A teacher who is unwilling to engage in a study of the community is likely to have a very limited impact on children. It is also quite likely that such a teacher's materials and approaches will lack relevance to the child's life. Furthermore, a teacher whose work is not relevant to his students' backgrounds is an incompetent instructor. As dismissal from teaching for

reasons of incompetence is not generally accepted by
the profession, however, there is no point to playing
this tune any louder.

Let us instead outline a procedure by which a perceptive teacher can learn about the community in which he
works. First-hand observations are essential, and here
the concept of research comes to bear. There is no
doubt that the neophyte teacher can learn much from
reading and university discussions about the subculture
of the poor, about ghetto life, or about the problems of
urban schools. It has been my experience in observing
teacher-training classes that even the best students are
limited in their perceptions if their knowledge is con-
fined to secondary sources. It is essential, therefore, that
at both the preservice and in-service levels of teacher
education the teacher be given the training needed to
study closely the area in which he is or will be working.

The case has been well stated by G. Alexander
Moore, who presents an anthropologist's model for
teachers to utilize while they seek to develop and analyze a personal teaching style. The model is also most
appropriate for community study activities. He writes:

> . . . Anthropologists and school teachers share one ob-
> vious feature in common, they both must continue to
> learn throughout their adult life. As the constancy and
> tempo of change in modern America continues to be-
> come more manifest, it is clear that all our professionals
> must know how to meet new situations. Who can say
> that in twenty years, or a generation hence urban schools
> will look anything like these shown here.
>   But the model of the anthropologist is more specifi-
> cally important to the school teacher. We are not sug-
> gesting that you acquire all the corpus of specialized

knowledge that an anthropologist must take years to master. Far from it. However they have certain tools of their trade that an urban teacher could use. These are people who know how to go into a foreign culture, present themselves straightforwardly to the new people, and learn from their new neighbors. Anthropologists enter strange cultures with very few preconceptions. First they are taught that they must respect, and if possible, like their new acquaintances. Beyond that very little is set. Although most anthropologists have some idea of problems they are interested in, they must be ready to abandon them if something more important or more germane to the lives of their people turns up. They know that they can never know beforehand what they may find.[1]

Moore notes that "it won't be easy," and we agree, particularly because the teacher must be able to control his personal value set. Without such an approach, however, the urban teacher is doomed only to fill a teaching slot, however well or badly, and to grow very little as a professional.

Finally, the term "study" in no sense implies a need for social distance between teachers and people in their community. A degree of social distance does exist, but one goal of the study is to help eliminate it. If this goal is not acceptable, little good can come from perfunctory community-study activities.

Conducting a Study

The first step in a community study is to define the school area. Needless to say, no school community is contiguous with the street boundaries served by the school. Yet it is the immediate area that is most amenable to study and thus where a start can be made. By means of walking and car tours of a given school area, one can make a tentative appraisal of a neighborhood in a relatively short time. Census tracts should be consulted to gather basic ethnic, racial, income, educational, and population data, which will provide a framework for further analysis. Census data are, of course, always out of date and must be interpreted in light of either later data or the teacher's personal observations. Any teacher who is willing to spend half a dozen afternoons and evenings traveling about a school area will begin to develop a realistic appraisal of housing conditions, recreational facilities, city services (police, fire, library), churches, industries, businesses, centers of congestion, public-health conditions, student hangouts, travel patterns utilized by students in coming to and from school, and so on. Tours should be made at different times of the day and week, so as to avoid a skewed picture of the area. A map of the area should be consulted and perhaps annotated.

But simply driving and walking about an area are very limited means for achieving insights. The teacher must also be willing to meet the people living in the area; anything less will be superficial and not worth the time spent doing it. We stress the walking and driving approach only because it is a start even the most timid teacher can make. Getting acquainted with some residents of the area is usually not too difficult. Ministers and priests, for example, are generally quite willing to host visitors and to talk about the problems and prospects of their church and its parishioners. The teacher certainly has every right to call upon police and fire-department officials or the public-health workers serving the area to learn about their work and to appraise their insights. Some of what one will hear will be the often biased traditional wisdom of these professions and occupations. The closer one can get to people living in the area, the more likely it is that a reality base will develop. If the person being interviewed, like the teacher, merely drives into the area to work, his impressions are quite limited. Generally speaking, civil-rights workers, leaders of black-nationalist groups, members of minority-group clubs, block-club leaders, and similarly involved people are far likelier to tell it the way it is. Being accepted by people in the neighborhoods is not easy. The upsurge in black-nationalist feelings, for example, will make it more difficult for even concerned white teachers to become better acquainted with ghetto conditions. Nonetheless, the need for a greater knowledge of and an involvement in community life places the responsibility squarely on the teacher.

Any public meeting in the area, whether it deals with politics, a community problem, or the celebration of some holiday, provides another opportunity for the teacher to meet people and to become better acquainted with them. The teacher also has entrée into some of the homes of the community. He has a professional responsibility to contact parents with whose children he is working. We must stress, however, that the teacher who is interested in learning about the community should make these home contacts to discuss the positive accomplishments of his students, rather than the inevitable problem cases, which usually offer the rationale for home contacts. The widespread expectation that a teacher's visit to a home is similar to that of the doctor or the police, that is, that there must be some trouble or he wouldn't have come, will take generations to break. But there is no reason why a concerted effort by teachers, within a given urban school over a relatively short period of time, could not begin to change this image. More than one school district has experimented with "friendly home visits." In these programs, teachers visit homes because they are interested in their students, rather than to bear tales of misbehavior and poor grades, which many parents have come to expect when a teacher calls.

If the teacher is indeed research minded, he will recognize that touring, visiting agencies, and talking to people can offer only fragmentary information about an area. It is unlikely that any teacher can undertake the types of social research that get to the roots of attitudes and behavior in an area. But there are not enough sociologists and anthropologists in the world to undertake the types of small-scale, action-oriented research activities that urban school personnel need. If studies are to be made of the hundreds of neighborhoods served by schools in any large city, teachers will have to undertake them. The perceptive teacher will learn that some people he contacts in the neighborhood are likely to be just as limited in their perceptions of the area as he is. It is likely that the teacher will begin to develop a cautious view of the varieties of feelings and attitudes found in the area. It would be foolish for a teacher who visited six homes in a neighborhood; who spoke to a police officer, to one minister, to three store keepers; and who drove about the area two or three times to feel that he knows all there is to know about the neighborhood. For all we know, this teacher may have spoken to some of the best or worst informed people in that community. One policeman, for example, does not represent the entire force in the area. Although he may reflect much of what his colleagues feel, there is always the possibility that he is an outsider to his own profession.

It is clear that, "right or wrong," any person's perceptions of the area in which he lives or works are legitimate and must be included in any systematic analysis. The degree to which a view is shared or contradicted by other sources is a key problem. The matter is further complicated by the teacher's own perceptions, which will often lead him to accept or reject the information he has gleaned on an unconscious level. If the teacher recognizes that there are limitations to what he can learn from scattered interviews and impressions, the community-study approach is sound. If the teacher accepts at face value his limited contacts, he is going to make many mistakes. It should be said in all fairness, however, that any teacher who makes the effort to get acquainted with the area, even on a limited scale, will no doubt have far more expertise than most of his colleagues do. He will find, unfortunately, that some of his peers will take a variety of negative positions on the community-study approach. Some will simply ignore, reject, or fight against any suggestion that they explore the area: "Don't bother me," "I don't want to know about this community," "I already know all I need to know," "You must be out of your mind to go out there," "Its not my job" exemplify some of the attitudes that will be uncovered.

One way of demonstrating what is involved in a community study is to examine the efforts of two young teachers who, as part of their undergraduate training, became acqauinted with a section of the city that was foreign to them. Let us turn to their analysis of their experiences and appraise the impact of their work.

A Community Study

by SUSAN DUBRINSKY
and SANDRA ACKER

A community study is an investigation of a specific area— in this case determined by school boundaries—focusing on the people who live and work in it, the types of businesses found in it, the services it provides and/or are provided to it, and the opinions of people outside of it. It involves walking around the area, noticing the way people look and act, and talking with as many different people as possible.

We made a six-week study of the community around —— School in conjunction with an education class, to research the people and their pattern of living so that if we ever taught in a similar community, we could teach with greater understanding. By explaining how we conducted our study, we have tried to indicate some of the things to look for, the types of people to interview, and several ways of conducting interviews.

Description of Area

We began by accumulating statistical data about the —— School community, which is close to the downtown area. Many years ago, wealthy people lived in the area; now it is inhabited by poor people, many from the Appalachian area of the South. According to the 1960 census, about 69 per cent of the area residents are white and about 30 per cent are Negro. About 12 per cent were born in another country. The school population is approximately 50 to 70 per cent southern white, 20 per cent Negro, and 3 to 5 per cent Chinese; the rest includes various nationality groups. In 1957, there were about 1,200 children enrolled in the school; in 1964, there were about 600 enrolled. There is also a high rate of transiency in the area. The school has a 100 per cent turnover of students every year, for although some children remain in the school for extended periods of time, others may leave and come back three or four times in one year. Each of these transfers in or out of the school helps to raise the exceptionally high turnover rate.

The people in the area live in hotels, apartments, or boarding houses. In 1964, there were only two integrated apartment buildings. Many buildings in the area are very rundown. According to one —— student, one abandoned house is "haunted," and people often climb in through a basement window to spend the night.

According to the 1960 census data, the range of rooms in each housing unit is 1.5 to 5.0. About 20 per cent of the housing units were deteriorated (there were signs of neglect which could lead to serious structural damage if not corrected) and 3½ per cent were dilapidated (not safe and adequate shelter). As part of urban renewal, some of the dwellings have been razed since the census. Rent in apartments ranges from $44 to $82 per month.

One person we interviewed termed this a declining area but mentioned that the parents do maintain the apartments fairly well. Another person pointed out that there is no place for the children to study at home. There are not many books in most of the apartments, but where there are books, the children do better in school. A teacher said that she could not send books home with some of the children because the books would be torn up. Another person called the homes "pretty deprived" and gave an example of a building where many apartments have no furniture, books, magazines, or pictures. A fireman commented that when fighting fires, furniture is saved if it is of any value; however, some of the people use orange crates as furniture.

We visited one apartment. The building in which it was located was very dim; it was difficult to read the apartment numbers. The apartment we visited did not have a number on the door (it had fallen off), and the lock was broken. The air in the hall had a very stale odor. The living room in the apartment contained a small couch and an overstuffed chair (both needing to be upholstered), two tables, a broken organ, a guitar, an ironing board with an iron on it, and a combination color television and radio. There were several prints on the walls, a mirror, and a mirrored knickknack shelf. The kitchen, which like the living room was very small, had an old, filthy refrigerator, a stove, a sink, and a table. Underneath the table was a box overflowing with empty beer bottles. We caught a glimpse of part of the bathroom. The bathtub was rather old-fashioned; it was the kind that stands up on legs. In the living room, we saw a few newspapers on the floor but no books.

There seems to be little space for the children to play. The school playground is very small and is locked at night. A church we visited has a small adjoining playground. We saw one "backyard." It was very small and narrow with little grass and much litter.

There are also many businesses in the area, including grocery stores, beauty shops, laundromats, pawn shops, loan companies, a manufacturing company, restaurants, a well-frequented skating rink, a university theater, and several retail stores. Located in this area is a large building which contains many social service agencies. Also in the area are a Salvation Army rooming house for elderly men, antique stores, and bars (including one which is very close to the school and features female impersonators). Along one street there are seven bars within five blocks. Other establishments include a Chinese Merchant's Association. Also in the area are many social service agencies and several churches. We saw no store-front churches in the area.

Procedures and Suggestions

Our investigating procedures varied according to the situation. In general, we combined interviews and observations. Whatever the approach, however, we found it necessary to remember to use tact, stay alert, and adapt to the situation. These are some general suggestions:

Let the situation determine the approach. It is advisable to make appointments for interviews with school-related personnel and neighborhood social workers. This ensures that the interviewee has ample time to converse and possibly can obtain some relevant printed material. In this situation, you can explain why you are there and take notes.

However, in some situations a nonstructured approach is preferable. For instance, walking into a neighborhood store and engaging the proprietor in casual conversation may yield valuable information. And when talking with a waitress at a hamburger stand, "just curious" may elicit more information that "We're from the University and we're writing a community study. . . ." In fact, we saw a woman alienated by this approach—this introduction caused her to become suspicious and to refuse to answer questions. If you're daring, you might try a novel approach. One girl tried to rent an apartment for herself and her three nonexistent children.

Sometimes it is better not to take any notes until you are away from your informant. At other times one person might take a few notes while the other keeps the conversation from lagging. Compare notes as soon as possible after an interview and write down as many details as you can remember.

Let the person converse freely. It pays to be patient even when the person wanders from the topic in which you are interested. Letting people talk about their own life histories and experiences may lead to what you want. For example, one woman gave us an extensive account of her history as a particular type of teacher. Our attention pleased her, and she then willingly gave us helpful information on her experiences at the school.

Have some questions in mind, but be flexible. Ask some general "warm-up" questions: "How long have you worked here?" "How do you like the neighborhood?" "What kind of things do you sell here?" "Do you know anything about the school?" Try to avoid asking too many negatively toned questions, although you may find some necessary to get a full picture: "Have you had any problems?" "Is this really a vice area?" In general, change your questions to fit the situation. The answer to one question will lead naturally to another question. Also, a conversation will be more valuable than an interrogation.

Leave a good impression. Common courtesy demands that you thank a person for his time and send a thank-you note for a prearranged appointment. Many individuals should not separately interview the same person. This happened at —— School after a teacher suggested that a storekeeper might be willing to talk to students. Needless to say, the man became very aggravated after about four visits. Courtesy will leave a congenial atmosphere for other persons undertaking community studies.

See as many people as you can and use a variety of techniques. People we talked to included those at neighborhood stores (photo, antique, dime store, restaurant), Neighborhood Service Organization (three workers), the assistant principal, the school-community agent, the visiting teacher, the remedial-reading teacher, the nursery school teacher, other teachers, the attendance officer, firemen, and children. We also visited club meetings and apartments and took walks around the neighborhood.

We have already considered some techniques, such as interviews and casual conversations. Attendance at club meetings of school clubs produces a wealth of material. Look over some of the children's records, but beware of taking them at face value. Accept all printed material you are offered. Background reading will give you greater insight. Snapshots, if you have the use of a camera, may capture not only interesting local sites, but also unexpected events. The best technique is to keep your eyes open. Notice details such as speech, dress, health, prejudices. Try to verify what you hear with actual observations; knowledge is always better than hearsay.

Compare your sources and evaluate your information to get a more accurate picture. Try asking different people the same question to see if you get the same answer. For example, people around the school disagreed about the reasons for the low voter turn out rate in the area. They agreed, however, that there were no gangs in the immediate area. Realize that information may be biased. One man told us that the neighborhood was mostly Negro— a conclusion easily refuted by simple observation.

Be aware of your own biases. It is all too easy to see things through a "middle-class screen." While investigating a lower-class neighborhood, we were continuously confronted with shocking, or at least surprising, facets of everyday life there. Let us cite some examples. —— does not have a P.T.A. We grew up in schools with P.T.A.s— they seemed an unquestionable fact of grade-school life, as integral as the school auditorium. The idea of a P.T.A. was rejected by parents, we were told, because of the difficulty involved in paying dues. We simply could not accept the nonexistence of P.T.A.

In a social-studies class, the teacher asked, "How many of you had breakfast this morning?" Not more than half the class raised their hands. And we must admit we were shocked upon hearing ten-year-old girls quite frankly discuss sex and the latest pregnancies and rapes in the area. And it was startling to see how impressed they were that we lived in houses—not apartments or hotels. When one of us was in a neighborhood church, a little girl came up and cajoled "Gee, I wish someone would give me a dime."

However, a key word of caution: Don't let your stereotypes determine your interpretations.

Organize your paper. There are many ways to organize a study. We suggest that you look over your notes first and try to find a unifying theme or a logical progression of topics. One possible next step is to write an outline and then arrange your notes in the approximate order of your outline. A sample format:

1. Introduction (including the orientation and purpose of your paper).
2. Description of the community (including the school area, businesses, area services, census data, a map).
3. Description of life in the area (a) comments and attitudes of school related individuals; (b) of nonschool-related people; (c) personal observations; (d) reactions from the children themselves.
4. Conclusion (including material from background reading, a summary of findings, an analysis of finding and examination of attitudes, values, and value changes).
5. Bibliography (all the sources you used) and Appendix (including such things as a list of places visited with dates, printed material, snapshots, etc.).

Enjoy yourself. This need not be a bothersome task. Rather, it can be rewarding, eye opening, and often fun. Keep an open mind and your sense of humor. Even if you intend to teach in the suburbs, don't be guilty of totally neglecting the "Other America."

Attitudes of Others

You will soon discover that a total picture of a community includes more than a list of facts or characteristics. When a person tells you about the neighborhood, he is telling you about himself. The attitudes and prejudices of those who live and work in the area are vitally important because they may be shaped by the conditions of the community and furthermore may have a determining effect on the future of the same community. For example, people moving into the area may meet the characteristics of it with disgust and consequently be apathetic toward efforts to improve it. Others with more sympathetic attitudes may be the first to initiate improvements. You might notice that attitudes fall into catergories such as sympathetic, unsympathetic, and mixed. Then you can analyze the reasons for each person's attitudes in terms of his connection with the community, his involvement in its activities, and his ability to reason clearly as shown by his other comments.

Most likely to be unsympathetic, we found, were those who resided elsewhere but whose work took them into this area. This is not a blanket rule, however. One of the persons most vehement in his anti-area comments was a resident, a man interviewed in a neighborhood hamburger stand. He commented that the area people were "atheists," "destroyers," "haters," "most destructive people in the world," and "immoral." He added that "Nothing can be done to help them," "The only way that they can be helped is by putting them in work camps and torturing them or killing them." Such a person is obviously unstable himself; as an estimation of the neighborhood, his remarks could be largely disregarded. The woman who owned this same hamburger stand, a suburbanite, was also quite vocal on the subject of this community. She accused the neighborhood residents of being unconcerned with education or voting and explained this by the fact that the people would be "better off down South." This woman could be regarded as an example of the many people holding stereotyped attitudes toward the in-migrants from the South.

A fireman told us that this was a terrible neighborhood —harboring bums, prostitutes, and lesbians—where the standards of cleanliness are "not the same as yours and mine." Since a fireman can reasonably be expected to have seen a lot of the area, such comments must delineate topics for further investigation, keeping in mind the sociologist's query—why do these conditions exist?

One attitudinal pattern that emerged was the tendency of those people closely associated with the school to be sympathetic. On the subject of voting, for instance, the school-community agent pointed out that "people on welfare feel they don't have the right to vote." She looked beneath the surface characteristic—lack of political interest —and partially explained it by poverty, frequent moving, and the lack of books in the home. In the same way, the assistant principal pointed out various patterns of disintegration in family life caused by the urban environment. He described the situation of a tightly knit family used to a rural, outdoor existence being cooped up in a tiny apartment without pets, hunting, or fishing. The father, low-skilled, finds it difficult to get a job. So the mother works at a low-paying job while the father either stays home and assumes the mother's role or drinks out his frustrations in nearby bars. The mother either struggles to bring up her family or gives up and joins the father in the bar. According to the school's visiting teacher, the children find life a great strain and tend to daydream. With so many cases of no breakfast and no one to see them off to school, the children are restless and inattentive in the restrictive world of middle-class-oriented education. "Yet," said the reading coach, "we impose a rigid academic program and expect them to react the way we did."

There is probably some truth in the comments of almost

everyone we interviewed. Probably the most sensible attitude is one of sympathy but realism. For instance, perhaps
it is true that some people waste money on beer instead
of books. And preschoolers aren't prepared with the conceptual skills necessary for reading. And a neighborhood
with cheap and dilapidated housing will naturally attract
undesirable people as well as poor in-migrants. But it is
only with the help of those more fortunate that people
will be given the chance to learn how to enjoy life without
excessive alcohol, how to make the most of abilities and
ambitions, and how to encourage their children to benefit
from the education offered them.

Our Attitudes

Our findings at the conclusion of our community study
took on added meaning when compared to our initial
attitudes and expectations. Since the school was located
not far from downtown in a depressed neighborhood, we
knew it was part of a so-called "vice area." Our mental
picture of a vice area included streetwalkers, dope addicts,
alcoholics, and criminals at every bus stop and a vague
fear of glowering giants with six-inch knives in their hands.
We also entertained the common conception of a poverty-
stricken community as all Negro, with the inhabitants all
subsisting on welfare. However, we did consider that the
assignment could hold the interest of a task.

Our parents reinforced our fears. They did not see how
the school could expect us to go into "that neighborhood";
our mothers worried "will you be safe?" One of us was
given a spray gun repellent to keep in her purse and told
not to stay in the area after 5:00 P.M. The attitudes of
the other students assigned to —— were similar; they were
nervous and uncertain. Some were also resentful and

narrow-minded. "I'm going to teach in the suburbs any-way," went one typical comment, "so why do I have to observe here?"

Our first in-person impressions of the area came on the day of our first assigned observation, when ——'s assistant principal took us on a walking tour of the neighborhood. This, in some ways, was an excellent introduction, helping us to fix the school boundaries and important sites in our minds, but unfortunately it also reinforced some of our preconceptions. We were especially shocked by the broken glass on the streets and the large number of dilapidated, boarded-up houses (and the knowledge that people found shelter in some of them). Neighborhood anecdotes also shocked us; for instance, stories of two prostitute mothers renting adjoining rooms, one for their children and one for business.

As a result, when we first ventured alone for the purpose of interviewing for our studies, we took precautions— the spray gun and a male friend. We began with a pre-arranged appointment at a company near the school. After this, we walked into several stores located on the same street as the school, and we talked to the owners. We also talked to one little boy. What did we see of interest? One (possible) streetwalker, lots of old men, and lots of children. No glowering giants—no knives. After this, we lost most of our nervousness, at least in the daytime. We have a more realistic impression of the neighborhood. It is not a desirable place to live—it is dilapidated. There are crimes; there are undesirable characters; and we heard remarks from passing youths. However, most of the people we met were friendly.

The children at first did not seem unusual, except for their southern accents. Later we could tell that some of their clothes had seen better days. For example, one girl often wore a dress that had obviously been cut down for her. It had a wide hem and was still too big. Some of the children do not have enough warm clothing for winter.

After we had been in the area for a while, we felt more sympathy than condemnation for the people. We found out that some of them did not always understand the ways of the city. They knew nothing about the different cuts of meat; they would eat uncooked spaghetti because they did not know it was supposed to be cooked; they did not vote because they did not feel they had the right to.

We found out that not all the inhabitants subsisted on welfare. One person told us of families she knew that would not accept welfare, even though it would have meant more money for them than they could earn at their unskilled labor. On the other hand, there were also cases of people who did not care. Some were more willing to have things done for them than to do them themselves.

We now have a greater respect for the people who live in the area and can see them as individuals, some of whom do care and want to improve themselves. We can also see that there is a strong need for people who can understand the residents of the community and help them. The —— school is fortunate to be a participant in the Great Cities School Improvement Project, which, among other benefits, provides additional trained school personnel to do this.

We now have a greater understanding of how projects like this might help over a long period of time. Since there are some people in communities like this who care, perhaps these people, with the help of social workers and school personnel, can help the community so that the children of those who are now children will have a better life.

Conclusions

We realize that a study such as ours only scratched the surface. It would take a great deal of intensive study to thoroughly understand the people and their problems. On the other hand, the experience of exploring an inner-city school and community is a tremendous eye opener. In particular, it offers an introduction to another style of life. It is common for a middle-class individual to entertain a mixture of stereotypes and prejudices with regard to inner-city inhabitants. As always, stereotypes will have a grain of truth. But unfortunately we often let this blind us to the larger picture of poverty, despair, and radically restricted opportunities.

It is typical for middle-class persons to feel that ambition guaranteees success, that anyone can go to college if he works hard enough. But what about the child who enters first grade scarcely having heard anything but terse commands, to whom teacher's long sentences are complicated verbal exercises, who isn't sure what square, round, up, down, above and below really mean. Educators are now claiming that age five or six is too late for a child like this to begin school—he lacks the conceptual skills to succeed in the primary grades and consequently begins a demoralizing sequence of failures until the college idea becomes ludicrous.

One must admit that there are some differences with regard to community and family structures in depressed areas and in the outer city or suburbs. First of all, the family in the inner city may consist of a mother supporting six children instead of the conventional mother, father, and two children. The mother is working, not because she wants a career, but because she must, even if the job only pays 80 cents an hour. Her preoccupation with survival precludes extensive interest in or encouragement of the children's work in school. With little money to spend and few material possessions, the children may dream of the day they can quit school and earn money—and the mother may even encourage this so that some of the burden is lifted from her. Without encouragement and example, the children concentrate on short-range rewards—the far-off benefits of schooling are remote.

This is the situation with which our schools and teachers must contend. It involves lack of preparation; lack of motivation; and, since teachers are largely from the middle class, a set of values and rewards different enough from their own to be perplexing. A child from a home which deemphasizes education will not always have great respect for teachers and authority. And if the teacher cannot win respect and attention, the classroom may become miserable for her and meaningless to her students.

A teacher, or for that matter anyone, must realize that these children are neither demons nor dregs of society, but children who haven't had breakfast, who don't go to the dentist every six months, who have cramped apartments for homes and glass and gravel for backyards, who never heard of a P.T.A., whose parents have never taken them to the zoo or read them a bedtime story or subscribed to *Life* and *Time*. We must face the fact that these are children entering the game with a substantial handicap.

It is natural to ask "What's being done?" Charles Silberman says that "no school in the United States has even begun to face up to the problem involved in educating Negro—or for that matter, white—slum youngsters." (Charles Silberman, *Crisis in Black and White* [New

York: Random House, 1964], p. 249). However, America is beginning to recognize its responsibilities in this field. Projects such as Great Cities, Higher Horizons, and Head Start are trying to open new vistas and enlarge the opportunity structure for inner-city children. But the need is so great that this may only be the proverbial drop in the bucket. These and other projects need even more public sympathy and always more funds. The problems of inner-city families and schools are so extensive and multifaceted that the programs dealing with them must be equally comprehensive. At the same time, they should be scientifically watched, organized, and evaluated so that educators can learn what really helps, what really motivates, and what is purposeless or harmful. There is a tendency to laud any attempt merely because so much is needed and so little is available. A modicum of success is better than none. We need more than this, however; we need long-range evaluation to see if there are optimum results.

Teacher training and teacher inducements must be re-evaluated. It is unrealistic to ignore the fact that the middle class teachers want to teach in the middle-class schools in the outer city and suburbia. It is difficult to blame them, either, for subject matter is taught and discipline is maintained more easily. Moreover, teachers rarely receive any real encouragement to teach in the inner city—there is no required "Methods and Materials in Inner-City Teaching" course. Consequently, beginning teachers feel unprepared to handle classes in these areas, and if they choose to teach in the city and are assigned to an "undesirable school," they may be faced with so many problems of a nature they do not understand and cannot handle that they too will escape to the suburban schools. It cannot be disputed that there is a need to face the problems of the city realistically, to be aware of population movements and of the middle-class "surrender" of the city to long-crowded Negro groups looking for better housing and better schools. A teacher prepared only to teach Dick and Jane is unprepared for the realities of city teaching. It is time for our teacher-training institutions to realize their responsibility to all children and to give prospective teachers the necessary understanding and skills for urban education.

Perhaps eventually the collective conscience of the nation can be sufficiently stirred to make greater and greater attempts to offset the harmful effects of a deprived environment. It is not a problem that will disappear if we ignore it; rather, like a toothache, it can only become worse. Education—compensatory education if necessary— can be the key to the improvement of society, if we recognize the need for immediate action.

*   *   *

An Appraisal

Let us examine a few of the ideas suggested in this evaluation of community studies. Our two young teachers certainly demonstrated the type of self-analysis that must be integral to any community study. Like any social scientist, they faced the need to examine their own expectations and attitudes as they reported what they saw. The end result is not value free and fully objective, but few things are. There is no doubt, however, that their efforts lean toward objectivity and that they are open to new data and to further self-analysis. Conducting such a study is therefore conducive to—but does not guarantee—better understanding of one's own premises and expectations.

The authors also make plain that pressures are put on the undergraduate or beginning student entering education who exhibits an interest in working in "that section of the city." Encouragement or discouragement is most likely to come from parents, husbands, boyfriends, other peers, teachers, and possibly university personnel. We might test the hypothesis that any familial and peer reactions to working in the inner city that the neophyte receives will be negative. As racial prejudice is one of the key divisive factors in our society, not to mention social-class, religious, ethnic, and occupational prejudices, it appears likely that most young people, long before they even consider becoming teachers, have already learned what sections of the city and what types of people they should "not get close to." Not that these attitudes are necessarily articulated by prospective teachers. Their vague projections of what teaching is simply do not include images of working with classes of Negro, Puerto Rican, or southern white children. We are dealing with untested hypotheses, but the pattern of avoidance is very real.

All that we can suggest is that any teacher who has any interest at all in teaching in the inner city must be aware of the probability of subtle efforts to dissuade him from his choice. Any teacher educator can cite the handful of students who are indeed dedicated and forthright in their reasons for choosing to be teachers in the inner city. The number of such young people is not great, however. The majority of people preparing to teach appear to have made up their minds, long before they entered their training, that they would prefer to

tcach in "nice" areas, which generally means areas with
green lawns and white residents. Even though efforts
are underway at some urban universities to redirect
teachers to the inner city, the basic facts of life in
teacher education have not changed. Most of our beginning teachers do not wish to become involved in the
inner city. Programs to recruit people to teach in deprived areas must be greatly expanded, and the programs
seeking to develop capable inner-city teachers need far
more support if the pattern of avoidance is to be seriously challenged. At this juncture, most schools of education have barely begun to satisfy the great need in
this area.

One obstacle to breaking the pattern of avoidance is
the middle-class fear of the inner city, noted in the appraisal of the community study and earlier selections. A
high percentage of young people entering schools of education are simply afraid of being anywhere near the
inner city. They may even fear attending an urban university, for it is too close to "those people." One reason
that the fear of the inner city is so strong is that most
people entering the teaching profession are women.
Women, in our society, are taught to be fearful of various groups and various sections of the city. Their fear is
deep-seated and very difficult to contend with. There
appears to be no way to overcome it other than by first-
hand experience with the inner city. When the neophyte teacher learns, as most will, that the "foreign"
sections of the city are not the jungles that they have
been led to believe and that they can walk about, shop,
and attend church in the area, they finally begin to op-

erate in a rational, rather than an emotional, way toward the inner city. As many teachers are unwilling or
are not expected to have even superficial inner-city contacts, a high percentage of them will select only those
incidents or information that reinforce their fears. They
will persist in clinging to their fears and nightmares of
working in ghettos or poor areas. Because our society is
so highly prejudiced toward the poor and toward dark-
skinned people, efforts to convince women that they
can teach in an inner-city area in perfect safety often
fail. In fact, these efforts are ridiculed on occasion. The
inevitable questions and challenges raised are heard
again and again: "Isn't it true that a teacher at such and
such a school was bopped on the head?" "Isn't it true
that a teacher at another school had her purse taken?"
"Isn't it true that a teacher at still another school had
his tires slashed?" "Isn't it true that 'everyone knows'
that school is a blackboard jungle?" These are only
a few commonly heard remarks. The people asking
these questions are often sincere, sometimes bigoted,
and certainly fearful. It is true, of course, that there are
incidents of violence in some schools, that there are
hoodlums who sometimes hang around a school, that
crimes are committed in every city, and so on. But it is
also true that the overwhelming majority of teachers in
inner-city areas go through the day without being
bopped, without being challenged by a hoodlum, without having their tires slashed, and without any incident
of this nature taking place. But these facts prove un-
popular among both teachers and the lay public. The
lay public simply feels it knows better—it *really* knows

what "those" schools and "those" kids are like. For example, I have had occasion to describe a typical day in an inner-city school to a group of outer-city dwellers, only to receive a reaction of complete disbelief. Most people simply don't believe that schools, regardless of their location, are more alike than different. They see the inner-city school as a hell hole, and nothing that can be said will change their minds. And some teachers are very unhappy working with lower-class or Negro children and will refuse to acknowledge the relative calmness in most inner-city schools simply because they are interested only in the problems, the potential violence, or the occasional violence that reinforces their position.

It is not possible for the lay public to visit the so-called inner-city "blackboard jungle" schools. It *is* possible for teachers to do so, either during their university training or once they are in the system. There is no guarantee of what the neophyte teacher will see when he visits a school or when he engages in an inner-city community study. There is always the danger that he will look for and see the types of behavior that he wants to see, that he expects to see, and that support his views of the inner city. Certainly he may see some unpleasant things; every major city in the world has sections that are to some degree reserved for various forms of vice. Crimes of violence occur daily; there are bars reserved for hoodlums, homosexuals, and the numbers game; prostitutes can be seen operating on the street; and so on. It is interesting to note how many teacher discussions focus only on the negative aspects of some neighborhoods. Somehow it must be made plain that these types of behavior are rejected by the overwhelming majority of inner-city residents. It must also be made clear that, if the neophyte teacher *wants* to see only the seedy side of life, he can do so. Our argument is that any teacher who seeks to examine the full spectrum of life in the big city with any objectivity at all will find a tremendous variety of life styles, aspirations, and problems. We can only cite again the overwhelming rejection of the poor and of minority groups in our society. Because this rejection is so all-pervasive, the reactions of many teachers are "understandable," that is, they are acting out what they have been raised to believe. One can only suggest that teachers, of all the professional groups, be given every possible opportunity to study those sections of the city with which they are unfamiliar so that their misconceptions can be challenged.

Still another factor needs analysis. The fact that some "unpleasant" aspects of life are concentrated in a given area should not be accepted as *prima facie* evidence that one cannot teach in the area. One frequently hears the rationalization, "I cannot teach there because of the terrible conditions around the school." There is no absolute connection between conditions around a school and what goes on in classrooms. Some teachers do wonders with their children despite community conditions. The quality of education in a classroom cannot be excused away by arguing that it is conditional on whether or not a prostitute walks the street in the area. Ludicrous as it seems, this type of reasoning is offered when some classroom procedures are questioned. The real question is "Do *you* want to teach in the area or not,

whatever the conditions?" Blaming the conditions for
one's decision simply begs the question. "Do *you* want
to teach there?" is a straightforward question that puts
to rest the usual excuse—its "the area" that keeps the
teacher away.

The "Some" Concept

We are not attempting to cover up the tragic aspects
of life in the ghettos of our nation. Our concern is really
with only one word, a four-letter word at that. We refer
again to the *some* concept introduced in Chapter 3. Any
teacher who engages in an objective appraisal of life in
the community in which he lives will find *some* people
on public assistance and others who reject such help;
some people who feel negative toward the school and
others who are strongly supportive; *some* unfit parents
and *some* very helpful and interested parents, *some*
shopkeepers who hate children and others who see
them as kids rather than hoodlums; *some* policemen
who understand only the seamy aspects of life and *some*
who are seeking to change the image of the police in the
area; *some* housing that is dilapidated and unfit and
some that people are working hard to maintain; *some*
houses of vice and *some* neighbors that complain of this
vice; *some* bars that cater to vice and *some* that seek a
"quiet neighborhood trade"; *some* slovenly housekeep-
ers and *some* that take great care in their housework;
some homes with no books and some with books galore;
some front yards that are littered and *some* that are well
kept; *some* neighborhoods that are better tended than

others; and so on and on. That the percentages of each of these and other aspects of life in an urban area vary from section to section should almost go without saying. The essential fact is that all these aspects will be found in any area, whether it be in the inner city or in the most exclusive suburb.

My experience has been that a rather large number of students who undertake community studies as part of their training come out of the experience with *some* of their attitudes toward life in the inner city changed. Many of them find people with whom they can identify and whom they can respect. Some students are repelled by what they see; others simply go through the motions of the study with no real commitment. The different ways in which students approach their assignments are a part of teaching, however, at the university level, as well as in the grade schools. There appears to be no viable alternative to personal involvement on the part of perspective teachers in a study of the community, despite the uncertainties of what is learned. Only when teachers feel that they can walk in and out of their school building, "hang around" after hours, visit one of the stores in the area, or make a home call as a routine part of life will there be *some* hope that the necessary change in attitude can come about. We are not suggesting that a teacher should not take any of the "precautions" that any other citizen takes in an unfamiliar area. An occasional "incident" does take place, though it is usually nothing more than a wolf whistle. Many neophytes, for example, do their community studies in teams, not only because they feel "safer," but because they also have a chance to talk about their experiences and to evaluate their individual perceptions. And it would be naïve indeed not to expect an unpleasant incident or two as one begins to explore the community and talk to its people.

Interestingly enough, the "wolf whistle" noted above may cause only mild annoyance (or delight) in a "safe" area. It may be interpreted as a prelude to rape and mayhem in the inner city. Two boys roughhousing after school are dismissed with a "boys will be boys" attitude in a white area, but two inner-city boys similarly engaged are perceived as "a gang of uncontrollable youth."

A key factor that must be constantly kept in mind is that the teacher undertaking a community study must in no way give the appearance of "slumming." This statement may sound obvious, but exceptions to the rule do occur. To avoid this possibility, it is essential to remember that no teacher or prospective teacher has the right to invade the privacy of people with whom he may be talking. Although most people are quite willing to offer information once they know who is asking, they are under no obligation to do so. The rule of thumb to apply is one's own sensitivity toward prying. Ask only what you would be willing to reveal about yourself. It is equally important to be prepared for the inevitable cry of some who disapprove of "callow, inexperienced young teachers running up and down unfamiliar streets, bothering people, probably doing more harm than good, pretending to be social researchers," and so forth. We assume that planning, tact, and a gradual building of a storehouse of competence are the foundations of a good community study. We have neither patience nor sympathy with those who feel only a "qualified researcher" should undertake such work, for, as we have already noted, there is no reserve of qualified researchers who can. Even more important, there is no substitute for the direct involvement inherent in these activities. It is the process of involvement that makes the difference. Involvement is the main ingredient in the school-community study; it may also be its main goal.

Probably no aspect of teacher reparation is less controlled than are students' attempts to become familiar with a new area of the city. The possibilities and probabilities of whom they will meet, how they will meet them, what particular bits of information or insight they will gain, how their experiences pass through their social-class grid of values and aspirations are all beyond the control of the instructor. At least two types of needs are evident here: the need to work carefully with students and teachers on the procedures of conducting a study and on the obligations of the researcher always to respect the rights of the people he contacts and the need to discuss and appraise the types of information gleaned, so that the student-teacher has an opportunity to think through what he may have reported. Despite the risks and lack of "quality control," no viable alternative to the community study is available. We can continue to ask our students to read all the available books on the inner city and the ghetto, to show them films, to take them on an occasional field trip, to bring in the various experts, and so on. All these efforts are in the right direction; all these efforts will reach *some* of the students, *some* of the time, in *some* way. But unless the new teacher has an opportunity to test what he is seeing and hearing through personal involvement, it is unlikely that these activities will have any more impact than many of the other academic experiences he has from kindergarten through graduate school. It is possible to gain some insights not only by conducting a community study but also by engaging in a tutoring activity or joining a neighborhood club or youth group in the section of the city where one will be teaching. Any and all of these approaches have their benefits and must be expanded as preservice and in-service activities.

Teacher educators who seek to implement such programs have a responsibility to help students make contacts and to be ready to confer with students to analyze their work. To repeat, this particular approach is not new and is generally accepted in teacher-education programs that seek to train urban teachers. Acceptance and implementation on a broad scale are two different matters, however. It is necessary to stress that the community study is still used only on a small scale, and it is safe to guess that most teachers still do not have such experiences prior to their assignment to an urban school. It is necessary, therefore, that school systems also encourage such studies on the part of teachers. Studies can be accomplished best if the system gives teachers time to make them. Released time from the classroom is required, and here is the point where the "era of good feeling" ends. The number of school systems that can conceive of teachers getting acquainted with their communities on school time are few. We are not saying that such activity is not encouraged after school or on weekends. In fact, many workshops will pay teachers to make home calls as part of a community-study approach. But until such opportunities are made part of the teacher's regular assignment, the school-community-study concept has a long way to go before it is fully accepted.

To sound a negative note, let us suggest that the neophyte teacher will be likely to find many an experienced teacher who will simply say that this business of working with the community is bunk; that the people in the area do not deserve what they are getting now; that they are not to be trusted; that you are taking your life into your hands when you visit any of their homes; and that all you will get for your trouble is an education in how mean and ugly life can really be when people are too lazy to help themselves. One can only guess how extensive this view is, but it does exist on every teaching staff, and it is part of the attitudinal underground of the school. Despite all the encouragement of a good principal and some universities and school systems do encourage teachers to become involved—the pressures of the underground are strong. We can only hope that the new teacher will be able to overcome negative pressure from some of his peers. He should seek out those who will support him and should ignore or resist those who will not.

As is no doubt plain, the essential purpose of the community study is to help penetrate the barriers or racial and social-class prejudice that separate too many teachers and schools from their communities. The study is thus a means to a more fundamental end. Such studies provide an academic framework within which the teacher may overcome some of his fears as he. meets people face to face. They are an alternative to passive acceptance of the need to learn about the community, as is urged in books or in one class or another. Granted, the studies will vary in quality, ranging from models of good survey research to superficial exercises. They will seldom be value free, but that is part of the learning process. They will often reflect the traditional wisdom of education. To cite only one example, absence of books in the home is repeatedly offered as a cause, rather than as a symptom of a more fundamental cause, for children's inability to read. Nor are studies a substitute for a deeper form of involvement. But they are at least a start. The irrelevance of much of what is taught in urban schools is still not really apparent to most teachers. Community studies should help them to recognize it.

Finally, we are clearly caught on the horns of a dilemma. Just as some small progress is being made in involving more teachers in school-community action, some spokesmen for the disadvantaged argue that they are fed up with being studied and are demanding more action to alleviate conditions. This view is acceptable as the logical outcome of many years of promises that have not produced sufficient results. The type of community study recommended here ought to help bring about closer working relationships between communities and their schools. It should also bring about better teaching practices and more appropriate curricula in the schools.

It is clearly a means to an end. If teachers find community resistance to being studied, then they have not made their goals clear. We are recommending not that people be studied as if they were objects but rather that they be given every opportunity to communicate their ideas to teachers and that everything possible be done to promulgate an honest exchange. If this is not the goal, community studies had best be forgotten.

Notes

1. G. Alexander Moore, Jr., *Urban School Days* (New York: Hunter College, 1964), pp. 270–1.

Chapter 6

Problems
and
Prospects

There are many reasons why people enter the teaching profession. Many teachers indeed want to teach: They have a concern for children and both drive and ideas. Others enter teaching for reasons that lead to weaknesses in the profession. There will always be some who use teaching as a "stepping stone." They have other careers in mind, but, as teaching is a relatively easy profession to get into, they work at the job while preparing for whatever else they have in mind. Many college women enter the profession simply because there is little else for them to do. Not that other professions are closed to women, for they are all opening, slowly but surely; but teaching is still the only profession, aside from nursing, that recruits mainly females.

When women marry, as most do, many of them leave the profession, causing serious problems of teacher turnover. Still others drop in and drop out of teaching throughout their lives, using the profession as a source of extra income. In a sense, teaching is a kind of pre-matrimonial limbo. And there are always the women who obtain teaching certificates as "insurance policies" when their husbands get close to retirement. The ease with which a teacher can enter and leave the profession at periodic intervals is a serious criticism of the skills required for teaching. If a teacher can pop in and out of the classroom over a number of years without becoming "dated," the slowness of change in educational practices is revealed as a patent fact. Such teachers are hardly professional educators, but they do "man" classrooms—and whether or not she can fill a required slot in a classroom is still the basic criterion by which a teacher is hired.

There are other reasons for entering and leaving the profession, many of them positive, but our concern is not with the usual pleas for better control of entry into the profession, although control is obviously necessary. We are mainly concerned with dispelling one myth about education, namely that teaching is a haven for the person who wishes security and an escape from life. The character of the profession is changing, and the demands on teachers have become and will continue to become ever more challenging. Anyone considering a career in education must recognize that his role will increasingly demand that he become involved in issues that are societal in nature and that he cannot escape behind the closed door of a classroom. Although the individual teacher's work with his class is still an impor-

tant criteria of his effectiveness, new developments in
team teaching challenge even this standard. We are entering an era when matching a teacher with twenty-five
to thirty-five children for a given period of time will not
be the only means of utilizing teacher talents. Technological change will also bring about an alteration of the
pattern. More important, teachers themselves are
beginning to admit that gross inefficiency and lack of
attention to individual differences are inherent in the
current structure of American schools. The profession is
complex and slow to change, however, and it will continue to need people to "cover" classrooms, no matter
how well or poorly. The need for a new breed of teacher
is clear, and we shall note some aspects of the life he
will be entering. Let us first examine some of the problems that demand a new type of teacher.

The teacher entering the urban school will quickly
learn that there are at least five major, all-pervasive
problems facing urban education. Once a teacher accepts a position in a system, these problems become
very real and immediate to him. He may, as so many
before him, try to pretend that they are "not part of his
job." The facts speak differently, however. Let us note
five of these problems or trends, not in any special
order, for they are all interrelated. The examination of
one is impossible without the stirring of others.

Mass Education and Staff Utilization

First and foremost, the neophyte teacher becomes involved in a system of mass education. Overcrowding is

simply a basic fact of life in urban schools. A teacher
will be inundated by swarms of children during his career. Despite efforts to reach individuals, most of his
decisions will be designed to move a group. Though
progress is being made in most systems toward cutting
class size, it will vary within each system. Some teachers
will work with groups of twenty, and others with groups
of forty, though the average in a given system may read
something like 32.7. Because education is a mass enterprise, because it is bureaucratic, and because there
is a tremendous pressure toward standardization in
organization, materials, and procedures, even the most
dedicated teacher will find it difficult to maintain his
drive and idealism. The physical and emotional drain
on teachers is a factor the neophyte must experience in
order to appreciate. And some of this strain is directly
related to the system, rather than to working with children. It is no wonder that many teachers retreat to the
position of saying "Give me a class, and leave me
alone." They honestly feel that they cannot handle the
broader aspects of life in a complicated school system.

Efforts to reform the system are constantly hampered
by teachers who withdraw their support and undercut
the efforts of others. We argue that, when teachers become students of the social system of schools and begin
to understand the nature of their bureaucracy, they will
then see ways to work in and around the system. We
hope that once a teacher can do so, he will feel less need
to retreat from the system. We need teachers who have
something to offer and who will make the effort to
achieve their educational goals. If we are talking about

part-time teachers, or teachers using the profession as a
stepping stone, or teachers whose major concern is with
doing as little as possible, obviously we are wasting our
time. That such people should be weeded out of the
profession, or relegated to relatively unimportant posts
within it, should go without saying. Unfortunately,
there are few efforts in this direction.

One way to encourage the good teacher and perhaps
rehabilitate the weak teacher, while at the same time
initiating the new teacher into the profession, is
through team teaching. Suggestions for new models of
staff utilization within schools, that is, for some teachers
to receive more responsibility and pay than others, seldom get very far. Team teaching is a step in this direction, for it recognizes the need for a team leader and the
gradations of ability among teachers. Despite many
"pilot programs" involving teacher teams, most teachers
are still expected to behave as they always have, that is,
to cover classrooms for the same pay, regardless of levels
of competence.

There is little doubt that American public education
is in a period of crisis. Although the system is obviously
functioning under adverse circumstances, minor modifications alone will not resolve the problems at hand.
There is an immediate need for changes in the ways
teachers and administrators apply their skills in the system. There is very little hope in the idea that the problems of mass education could be solved if only there
were more teachers. Obviously, if class size were to be
cut in half throughout the country, we would need approximately twice as many teachers. To cut class size

and then have the teachers do exactly the same things that they now do would be a tragic waste of both human energy and finances. Certainly, classes of thirty-five and forty should be reduced. But what then is the question?

What is desperately needed and what is on the horizon are ways to utilize faculties so that the traditional "lockstepping" of one teacher to *x* number of children is no longer the only formula that counts.[1] With every effort to bring paraprofessionals into education, the great potential of teachers working with teams of paraprofessionals in providing diagnostic and relevant learning experiences becomes more attainable. Not only can paraprofessionals help schools to overcome shortages of personnel, but new openings in the profession will offer opportunities for noncollege-bound people, a case well made by Frank Riessman and Arthur Pearl.[2] The use of paraprofessionals encourages differential use of school personnel. Team-teaching variations, using both professionals and paraprofessionals, offer a major hope for breaking the rigid compartmentalization of teachers and students so ubiquitous in the school system now. The team approach also provides the flexibility necessary to use new teaching technologies. The teaching machine, a generic term encompassing everything from simple forms of programmed instruction devices to computer based instruction, is here, but it has not yet been accepted by most educators. As Charles Silberman makes clear, many problems must be solved by merging the new hardware of electronic technology and the software of content and methodology.[3]

Nonetheless, the enormous possibilities for finally making individualized instruction an attainable goal, rather than a hackneyed tenet of education professors, have caught the imagination of the profession. It is significant that the impetus for the new technology is coming mainly from outside the profession, that is, from industries that see the great market for their wares. The educators spearheading the need for technological innovations are radicals within the profession, and they have yet to carry the day. Certainly few schools of education, if any, are preparing teachers for classrooms that will be much different from the model perpetuated over the last century.

Expecting teachers to adjust to team teaching (especially to performing before one's colleagues), to accept new technologies, and to work with paraprofessionals, without intense programs of in-service retraining, is unrealistic. Team teaching can contribute to retraining by bringing together the new breed of teachers and the veterans. Each group will learn from the other, but the greater need is for the experienced teacher of the traditional model to learn from the young teacher, who is prepared, hopefully, for a new type of schooling. Team teaching may also help challenge a serious problem within the profession, which may facetiously be called the "sweet-young-thing syndrome." As we have already noted, many young women entering the profession want to marry and have children. These women are, at best, part-time professionals, and using them on teams may help to reduce the disruptions now caused by periodic withdrawals to raise families. Team teaching may not be the best answer to this problem, nor will it overcome both the overcrowding or the dull repetitiveness of many classrooms in urban schools. But because it offers a flexibility of staff utilization now lacking and redefines the kinds of skills required of a teaching staff, it is a major breakthrough. Unfortunately, the resistance of experienced teachers to team teaching is strong, and newcomers to the field will probably also be conditioned to similar resistance.

If new patterns of staff utilization and new technologies of teaching ever do catch on, a better answer to the problems of mass education will be found. We certainly need more teachers, but to continue to expect them all to do pretty much the same thing is folly. It is a folly practiced by virtually every major school system, and the attempts to break the traditional pattern have not yet had any appreciable impact.

The Civil-Rights Revolution

Another major fact of urban life is the civil-rights revolution and its efforts to truly integrate America and its schools. The record of most American teachers in the civil-rights revolution is hardly outstanding. One can perhaps understand why so few teachers have become activists in that revolution. If teachers indeed represent the middle class and if being middle class means supporting the *status quo*, then teachers' reluctance to be identified with what has become known as the "protest movement" is predictable. Teachers are by tradition bearers of culture and are not expected to lead revolts.

Understandable or not, the unwillingness of most teachers to become involved in the civil-rights fight merely hampers what will eventually take place. It is unthinkable, given the events of the 1950s and 1960s, that the civil-rights revolution will not have a permanent impact on education, employment, housing, and other aspects of our life. Most teachers deserve little credit for these gains.

The pressures for a truly open society are mounting and will not go away. School systems will continue to find themselves in public conflict with the people seeking desperately to improve our society until schools exert a forthright leadership role on civil-rights issues. Progressive school systems will be attacked by those segments of our society that cry for gradualism, but at least schools will then be joined by people who view the goals of a democracy as open rather than limited or closed. Trends suggest that suburban schools will soon feel the demands for an open society; and for some teachers there will simply be no place to hide.

One could make a case for what some educators have been attempting to do in the area of equal rights for generations. One could also make a case for the programs that most major school systems have launched to help disadvantaged children. The objectives of these programs are closely aligned to some of the goals of the civil-rights movement. Changes in curricula did *not* come about because most teachers pressed for them; they evolved because of the pressure on educators and on urban schools from civil-rights groups. As Frank Reissman points out in one of his speeches, some educators have been discussing the inadequacy of the "Dick and Jane" type of primer for thirty years.[4] It was only after civil-rights groups demanded that books become more attuned to the facts of urban life that a handful of "urban readers" were finally written. Although educators blame publishers for the lack of intergrated books and vice versa, the rationalizations implicit in these excuses are too transparent to warrant discussion.

The new teacher must understand that he will be either for or against efforts to improve the political and social conditions of this nation. Educators are finally beginning to learn that there is no middle ground on these issues. They have long insisted that if they remain impartial and expound "both sides" of issues, they will be doing their job, whether it be in the classroom or on the public forum. Many educators will continue to take this stance. Although we are not suggesting that teachers become propagandists, how they handle the civil-rights question in their classroom is related to their values and their skills in eliciting discussion and interest on the part of students. We are concerned here with what teachers do to help or impede the efforts of civil-rights groups as these groups make their demands upon the schools. Too many teachers look upon these demands as inopportune, impatient, unrealistic, and so on. These same reactions are voiced by the body politic. Although not all civil-rights groups are pristine in goal or deed, their major goals are clear-cut. In short, there is no question as to who wears the white hat if one accepts the Bill of Rights at face value.

Teachers can make a vital contribution to the work of

the civil-rights movement by becoming involved in it. This involvement may be as minimal as attending some meetings and learning what is really behind the issues. It may mean becoming the school representative of a given civil-rights group, so that the group has access to someone who will speak frankly about conditions in the schools. We are clearly urging that teachers become far more involved in the civil-rights movement than they are now. We believe that any teacher entering the urban schools who is not willing to take this step will be of little use in the schools. Ours is an extreme position, and its validity has yet to be tested. Nonetheless, until civil-rights workers feel that most teachers are as concerned as they are about the issues of integration, conflict between the civil-rights movement and the schools will continue.

Teachers can hide behind a host of rationalizations about why it is not appropriate for them to become "involved." Such reactions only reinforce what we have suggested before, that is, that the majority of teachers enter the profession for reasons not conducive to experimentation, innovation, or commitment. They become parts of the system, and the price they pay is the avoidance of conflict. Most teachers and most urban school systems retreat in the face of societal pressures, rather than exhibiting the types of leadership needed to alleviate these pressures. School systems and teachers are thus on the defensive most of the time. To digress into a discussion of the variety of positions within civil-rights groups would only cloud the main point. The cries of "Get Whitey" expressed by the most militant black

nationalists are noted by some as a reason for avoiding
the civil-rights struggle, but it is likely that this avoidance was as pronounced when the struggle was more
moderate in tone. Teachers, on the whole, avoid civil-
rights issues and groups like the plague. Even in predominantly Negro schools, one finds many teachers denying
social reality and educating for an all-white world. It is
no wonder that conflict between educators and civil-
rights groups is too often the rule. Universities and their
schools of education are not excluded from this discussion. Although a remark by Abraham Bernstein is related to our next point, it is equally appropriate to link
it to the role of educators at all levels *vis à vis* the civil-
rights movement. He writes:

> Teacher training institutions, like all collegiate institu-
> tions, usually are demure, shy, and even in default on
> their public responsibility to clarify issues and policies.
> Consider the muteness of the teacher training institu-
> tions, public and private, when teachers strike, whether
> in New York or Utah. The silence is thunderous.[5]

The conservatism and timidity of most educators are
clearly social facts.

Teacher Militancy

Still another fact of life in the public schools will
sound almost antithetical to the foregoing statements.
In recent years, teachers in some larger school systems
have become very militant in their demands to become
partners with boards of education in the operation of
the schools. A decade ago, the suggestion that teachers

would have the right to collective bargaining in the near future was dismissed as union propaganda and inconsistent with the "true professionalism" that characterizes teachers. The transition to militancy has not swept the profession, however. Although every year more and more teachers are willing to take their demands into the streets, the majority of American teachers have not yet had their baptism of fire on this issue. There is little doubt that the teachers entering the profession in the next decade will become involved in efforts to strengthen it and to achieve a share in decision making. Many teachers have learned that in a pluralistic society organizational strength is the only real source of power.

There is no inconsistency in stating that, although most teachers have avoided involvement in civil-rights and political movements, more and more of them are becoming militant in efforts to improve teaching conditions and increase salaries. The new-found militancy of teachers has many overtones, and there is no question that some teacher leaders are also seeking to involve the profession in the civil-rights struggle. Witness, for example, the efforts of the American Federation of Teachers to help develop freedom schools in the South and to seek the introduction of Negro history classes, as well as other programs, in the North. The National Education Association is also making moves in this direction. Nonetheless—and this is admittedly a debatable view—the major goal of teacher militancy has so far been to improve the salaries and working conditions of teachers. Much energy is also expended in factional feuds among rival teacher groups. Little time or energy has been left for seeking ways to improve the quality of education in the schools. Professional leaders will argue that they *are* making such demands in their contracts and that, unless teacher working conditions are improved, there is no hope for the development of quality education. This point is acceptable here, but it is clearly tinged with the emotional overtones that permeate much of the debate about the new militancy.

The point we are making here is that the new teacher will probably no longer be able to say, "I will teach for a few years and see what the professional organizations have to offer before I decide which one of them I might join." The impetus of militancy as well as the reactions to it now force each and every teacher to take a position. We approve of this situation, for it has instilled in the profession a vitality that has not existed before. Which group is "right" is not an item of concern here. Our task is simply to suggest to the neophyte that he *will* be taking sides and that he *will* become involved. The neophyte who seeks to retreat from life, from issues, and from problems will find teaching in the urban schools a most frustrating task. If he is a person who accepts some conflict and controversy as a part of life, he will find a ripe field in which to test his ideals. The strife within his profession alone will offer many challenges. He will be part of an era when the professional image of the teacher may be based on *teacher* qualities, as well as on *teaching* qualities. There is a possibility that teacher militancy may help to bring about some of the more fundamental reforms needed in the public schools. Most school boards and administrative hierarchies have not brought about serious reforms. Perhaps, as teachers focus hard on their own working conditions, what we subject children to will also be exposed. At least, that is a hope. But, even if it does not come true, teachers are now taking the first major strides toward becoming true professionals. The teacher entering the profession in this era will have a better image of himself than did his predecessor only one generation past.

The Financial Crisis

A major crisis facing the urban schools is a financial one. Every major school system in the United States has a constantly expanding budget as urbanization becomes the essential pattern of life. Teachers quickly learn that, whenever they make a demand and whatever they would like to do, the standard retort they receive is "It costs money!" With the advent of some Federal aid, slight progress has been made in recent years. As long as most school systems depend on variations of the property tax for support, however, they will never really be out of the red. The same is true of all our public enterprises, and, as John Kenneth Galbraith has pointed out, the nation has yet to decide to spend more on the public sector of life than on the private. Such generalizations open another set of complex issues and arguments. Indeed, viewing teaching as very secure work is no longer feasible. The economics of the situation are such that even school systems can go bankrupt. Battles over integration in the South, for example, exemplify the position some legislators will take in cutting funds to schools that move "too quickly" in the desegregation crisis.

Teachers are not going to solve the financial problems of the schools, though their organizations can certainly make a contribution. Our point is that the urban teacher will find his career and his efforts to work with children very closely related to the public support that schools receive. If a teacher takes the position that he has no business working for greater public support, he will be contributing to the financial downfall of the schools. If, on the other hand, he is willing to become involved in efforts to win tax elections or to influence legislators, he will make his contribution to resolving the problem. There is a great need for teachers to unite in efforts to build public financial support. Progress in this direction has been made in the last decade, as teachers in many urban school systems have learned that they can help to implement campaigns for funds. Other teachers have yet to learn that these activities are necessary; they still do not want to become involved in the "dirty business" of politics. The neophyte who assumes this position and avoids the political aspects of his career will find that urban schools will not be a satisfying place for him. He will not be amenable, for example, to running for, or backing teacher candidates for, positions on school boards. Yet this type of political activity is vital if the financial crisis is to be tackled. Needless to say, because local authorities are generally unable to support schools and most other public services, except at minimal levels, the need for greatly expanded Federal expenditures is obvious and will not be elaborated upon.

The Disadvantaged Child

We have already noted efforts by public schools to meet the needs of disadvantaged youth. These efforts constitute the recognition of another major problem in urban schools, one that is closely related to integration efforts but is not restricted to civil rights alone. It has become increasingly obvious that efforts to educate disadvantaged children more effectively are also desperately needed to reach the majority of children in *all* schools. Teaching materials and methodologies that are relevant to life situations are as necessary in suburban middle-class schools as they are in ghetto schools. The new teacher will learn that his school system is likely to have launched hundreds of special projects designed to educate disadvantaged children more successfully. They range from preschool projects like Head Start to motivational projects like Upward Bound and will reach to such college-level programs as the Higher Education Opportunities Act. In many urban schools, the teacher will find opportunities to take part in a wide range of compensation or enrichment programs, from tutorial classes to after-school clubs.

One of the fundamental characteristics of the compensatory efforts is that they are not likely to upset the ongoing program of classes and time schedules. It is not surprising that many of these programs are developed for implementation on a summer or after-school basis. Here, unfortunately, is the best evidence of the entrenched patterns of organization and curriculum that characterize most urban schools. The traditional programs are generally inviolate, though here and there a few cracks are beginning to show. These cracks are appearing partly because many teachers are taking part in the compensatory programs—both on voluntary and paid bases—and they are beginning to examine some of their more routine practices as a result. As compensatory-education programs increase in scope, the probabilities are that they will begin to have a greater impact on the "regular school day." The urban teacher who teaches the same old material in the same old way year after year but then teaches an after-school class with new material or with a more sympathetic ear for his students, deludes only himself when he argues that after-school attitudes cannot be implemented during the regular school day.

They cannot be, it is true, unless the teacher is to some degree an innovator. The pressures and demands of the school day make it very difficult to break the mold. Perhaps the experiences that the teacher will have in the special activities will encourage him to alter his regular program. Though seldom discussed publicly, many after-school programs aim to bring this change about. The programs are always based on the argument that they will help children. Certainly, that is their *major* goal. At the same time, however, the opportunities for in-service education are also implicit in each and every one of them. The perceptive teacher who wants to test his ideals and his training will be well advised to get involved in some of the compensatory programs as soon as he can. He may well find a freedom that the daily grind of crowded classes tends to limit.

As we have noted, all these problems and trends are intertwined. Some teachers find change overwhelming and feel that their only recourse is to retreat from any type of involvement. Given their prior experience, training, and conditioning within the system, their reaction is not surprising. It is also not surprising that many urban-school administrators plead for teachers who are willing to try out new approaches and techniques. Each new teacher is their hope; they hope that he will be representative of a new breed of teacher. There is little reason to believe that a new breed is on the way, but at least their desire is a positive sign.

One final point should be discussed here. Any teacher fully committed to equalizing educational opportunities for disadvantaged children cannot ignore the present inadequacies of compensatory education. Research, particularly the recent nationwide Coleman study, suggests that the most powerful and effective equalizer in the present structure of education is the mixed-class, integrated school.[6] In light of this hypothesis it is apparent that teachers concerned with the culturally disadvantaged must become involved with both civil-rights programs and curricular innovations.

The New Breed

There is a vital need for a new breed of teachers. The profession has always needed more people who are interested in becoming *professional* teachers. We shall not find such people until two major transformations have taken place in the urban school. One change involves staff allocation within the schools; the other relates to the process of teacher training. Let us examine the training facet first. Much of the debate and rancor focused on teacher education in the United States attacks the quality of the education courses and submits as an alternative a stronger dose of liberal-arts courses. Both premises are wrong. That there are weaknesses in education courses cannot be disputed, just as there are weaknesses in all university courses if the same criteria for criticism are applied impartially. What is needed in teacher training is a far more realistic preparation for the tasks teachers face. It is often said that some education courses provide the teacher with ideals and seek to make him an introspective person but that they fail to provide him with the "know how" necessary for the job. Both attributes are vital, but the "know how" dimension is often short changed. There will be some student-teaching activities in most training programs, and thus the neophyte does serve a brief apprenticeship. Student teaching tends to be fruitful if the neophyte can adjust to the demands of one or more supervising teachers; if he can learn to control student groups; and if he has the ability to handle some materials, to promote continuity from day to day. As is well known, once his training is "complete," the neophyte is pretty much in a sink-or-swim position in the schools. The university has finished with him once he is graduated, and the school system is mainly interested in his "covering" a class.

Despite all types of in-service efforts and other internal efforts of the system to help the neophyte, the overwhelming experience is still a trial by fire. The teacher is expected to handle a group of thirty to forty children, hopefully in a subject area for which he is prepared. And that is just about all there is to it. Although the principal or assistant principal might walk by the class a few times, as long as the children are not climbing the walls and the teacher keeps his problems to himself, it is assumed that he is doing an "effective job." Education is a profession in which the first-year teacher is asked to perform the same tasks and exhibit the same skills as the twenty-year veteran. There is a tremendous need, therefore, for teacher-preparation programs to accomplish two tasks: to train neophytes in the skills essential for teaching and to relate this training closely to apprenticeship programs in the schools.

Teacher training must go far beyond mere discussions of what the "art of teaching" is like. It must include systematic training in the various skills required for planning and creating materials, for presenting materials, and for effectively managing groups. From the control of voice projection to audio-visual techniques, good teaching calls for many skills. And none is more important than an awareness of interpersonal relations.

Myth has it, among both professional educators and the lay public, that a good teacher is born, not made. To put it another way, if one cannot learn to interrelate with people or if one does not have some magic spark of greatness, he will be simply a routine teacher.

To accept this view is to reject much of what is known about personality development and the ability to learn. When and if most colleges of education take full responsibility for their products, a new breed of teachers will emerge. Many of the people who are now accepted and simply pass through schools of education should never enter the profession, except perhaps as subprofessionals. But for those students identified during the training process as having the potential to become good teachers, the rigor of any good program will stress demonstrable skills, a step that will certainly produce a smaller number of mediocre teachers. Unfortunately, the development of demonstrable teaching skills is not fully accepted by professional educators as a goal of teacher education. Aside from talking about innovation and desirable techniques, the responsibility for skill training is left pretty much to some type of student teaching. Student teaching may help to develop teaching skills, but there are far too many loose ends in existent student-teaching programs to warrant any satisfaction with the current state of affairs.

Even if colleges of education should raise their expectations and tighten their procedures (and there are some signs that they are beginning to do so), the training will be largely unavailing unless school systems look upon the new teachers as apprentices rather than as finished products. Every first-year teacher should serve an apprenticeship within the schools, and every effort should be made not to cut the apprentice adrift until he is fully prepared to handle the job. Many models are proposed for how school systems and universities can work together to provide the support for the neophyte teacher in the first year of teaching. Most of these models call for team arrangements, where one or several neophytes work with a master teacher. The neophytes' work is constantly being appraised, and they are given many opportunities to test and retest their teaching abilities.

As we have noted, schools should organize their staffs in teams, so that the capabilities of each teacher are utilized to best advantage. It is simply wasteful, inefficient, and ignorant to continue to push teachers into the breach, as if they were cannon fodder, year after year. Certainly, some new teachers will succeed and will become effective. But many others will learn to become very poor teachers, reinforcing the stereotype of the teachers who "keep school." Others will become disillusioned and will drop out of the profession. The need for well-trained people is far too great to permit the weaknesses of the present pattern to continue. When the major school systems of the nation recognize that the answer to the demands of mass education is not simply more teachers but instead a more intelligent use of the teachers we now have, some progress will have been made.

Many plans to achieve this recognition have been suggested, but we are not concerned with their details at this time. Our point is to suggest to the neophyte that either he or some of his peers will be the products of new training programs that will be different from what has passed for teacher training for some generations. It is also conceivable that he will enter a school system that will accept the responsibility for the in-service training necessary to make him a professional. The odds still are, however, that he will have only an introduction to teaching in his college work and that he will be cast adrift in his first year. If he recognizes this possibility, he may at least be psychologically prepared to cope with the situation. He may be more amenable to taking advantage of the opportunities that school systems offer for in-service training. When school systems begin to use fully the services of master teachers, sub-professionals, teacher aides, and a variety of staff adjuncts, the new teacher will finally begin to behave professionally. Then efforts to individualize instruction and to reach the disadvantaged child, and all children, will begin to bear fruit. In short, only when individual attention is given to teachers and teaching teams will the flexibility now largely absent in school systems become a realizable goal. And only when flexibility is an integral characteristic of the system can meaningful instructional changes be made.

The public schools are a long way from making these fundamental changes. There is no reason to expect that the public, teacher's organizations, or community groups will fully support suggestions to modify schools seriously. There are a host of reasons why people within a given social institution resist change in that institution.

Some efforts are underway in most systems to challenge
the old patterns, however. If the neophyte is prepared
to join efforts to change our system of education funda-
mentally, he may be able to make some contribution to
change; at least he will not hinder it. We are stating in
every way possible that the neophyte teacher is entering
a system in flux; a system that is both overwhelmingly
traditional and yet to some degree innovative; a system
that is being challenged to change by both professional
educators and by groups outside education; and a system
that is completely involved in the major social issues of
our day. It is a complicated system, and it calls for much
energy and effort on the part of people working within
it. The question to the neophyte is Will you be one of
those "who cares" and will do his part, or will you be
another "hanger on"?

We are not suggesting that the neophyte must
become a twentieth-century Renaissance man, able to
cope with each and every one of the challenges, problems, and opportunities presented by urban schools.
We recognize that each person will specialize in only
one or two aspects of the problems we have outlined.
We expect that most teachers who "care" will be concerned most about their children. If they are committed
to the welfare of their students, then other prospects
are also bright. But the cold fact is that many teachers
have lost this initial concern, especially when disadvantaged children are concerned. We have stressed again
and again that some teachers have given up, partly because the system has conditioned them to giving up,
partly because they do not really care about children,

and partly because their teaching skills are at a minimal level of competence. To them teaching has become a job. But even focusing on the children is not enough. The neophyte will also have to take on some broader professional problems. Whether it be the financial crisis, the civil-rights crisis, the in-fighting among professional groups, or the compensatory education programs around him, he will have many opportunities to make some contribution to the profession and to his own growth. If the neophyte does not become involved, he will still be able to earn a living and may get some satisfactions out of the job, but the probabilities are that he will become greatly frustrated.

Frustrated or not, he may well be considered a valuable teacher for two sad but pressing reasons: Teachers are needed to keep classrooms "covered," and there are relatively low expectations about what teachers should teach children. If a person does a mediocre job but meets his classes regularly, if he makes some attempt to teach (for example, "Read pages 117 to 121 and do questions 1-12"), if he fills out the appropriate forms and takes hall duty, and if he never gets involved with drinking on the job, patting boys or girls on the behind, or civil-rights activities, the odds are that he will survive for some forty years in the profession. His contribution to children, to the school, and to the system will be minimal, but he will still get his pension. If these statements sound pessimistic, they are not so intended. They are straightforward enough, however, to indicate what kinds of people we believe to be undesirable in the urban school.

What educators believe to be desirable or undesirable has very little to do with what will actually come to pass. It would be more realistic to say that, over the next decade, the types of people entering the profession, the types of training they will receive, their experiences in the first year, their attitudes toward the disadvantaged, their involvement in community affairs, and so on, will be much like what they are today or were twenty years ago. If a new breed is coming, it will permeate systems very gradually, as certain changes in both training and school systems take place. Idealistic hopes for better days in the profession must be tempered by a geologist's patience, whether we like it or not. The tides of change are affecting the profession, however. Innovations are underway on many fronts. Some writers prematurely suggest that education is in ferment. There are some good signs, and perhaps the pace of change is increasing. Changes in everything from teacher training and curriculum materials to programs for reaching the disadvantaged are being suggested, tested, and criticized. Federal funds for a variety of programs have helped to promote many new departures. Some innovation will come out of all this. But, even if a new breed of teacher evolves along with it, the evolution will be slow. The only point in discussing the possibility at all is to alert the neophyte that he will be a part of this evolutionary process. Indeed, he may well be able to move with it and help to expedite it. If he decides that he cannot operate in such a system, then his absence from the profession is no great loss. The profession already has enough people who have given up on the children they teach and who are stultified in their role as teachers. The profession needs fewer rather than more of these people. It desperately needs teachers who may be willing to conform to the system to some degree but who will also see the opportunities for innovation within it; teachers who will not become discouraged as they come up against the bureaucratic "slaps in the face" that are characteristic of a massive enterprise; teachers who understand the bureaucracy well enough to know how to operate within it.

In a sense, we need more "operators" in the system. Some of us who remember Sergeant Bilko of television fame may recall him partly as an unsavory character; but all would agree that he knew the army—he knew the system and how to beat it. To beat the system, however, does not mean that the system is necessarily an enemy. There is no question that Bilko loved the army, despite his plots. In the same vein, we are not seeking teachers who will fight the system just for the sake of fighting it. We are seeking people who will understand the system well enough to know that it grinds slowly and that it is impersonal, both to children and to its staff. But a system is also man made, and as such it is open to intervention. We may thus dismiss the term "operator," which most educators will reject as unsavory, and substitute the term "intervener." The opportunities for intervention are legion: The breaking of the textbook barrier, the utilization of materials appropriate to each child's abilities, the utilization of the new technologies of teaching, the challenging of rules that have lost their origins in antiquity, the exploration of new subject areas and questions usually not taught in school, the constant search for relevance in forms or organization, the promulgation of integration and the lessening of social-class bias, the challenging of the lockstep nature of virtually all school activities are but a few tasks awaiting willing minds.

The Need for Activists

Despite the need for young activists in the profession to counterbalance the pressures toward conformity, it is not likely that many people who are active in civil rights and related causes will be attracted to teaching. There are two fundamental reasons why. First, entry into the profession requires enrolling in a school of education. To those intimately involved in the process of teacher training, it is apparent that few students preparing to be teachers are the types of people who actively engage in civil-rights campaigns, campus demonstrations, or political activities of even the most routine and generally acceptable nature. Not that all students entering education lack social ideals. Some are indeed engaged in intellectual pursuits that bring them into contact with the more active students on a university campus. These people are rare, however.

There are many good people who wish to become teachers, but not many of them would be properly labeled "activists." A type of intellectual snobbishness is another reason why some of the more liberal students on campus avoid schools of education. Schools of education represent one of the more conservative elements of the university, though most other colleges and divisions are not really much more liberal. In fact, schools of education are more likely to develop introspective students than are some other professional schools. Much of the debate and activity within schools of education are dedicated to the need for innovation and change in school systems. This encouragement of innovation, however, does not extend much beyond the college classroom. To defend schools of education is not necessary here, for the entire book is based on the premise that such schools have a vital role to play in the preparation of teachers. At the same time, the image of conservatism that schools of education radiate does little to attract students who might be eager to take part in the debates and action-oriented programs necessary within the educational establishment.

There is a second reason that activists are not likely to be attracted to teaching. After all, it is possible to enter the profession after only minimal contact with a school of education, so the first reason can be circumvented. The activist who wants to get a taste of teaching can probably get one of the various types of provisional certification that permit him to substitute, especially in urban systems that hire any warm body as a substitute teacher. Here again, the image of the school and of school systems tends to repel the activists. If schools of education are conservative, most school systems are in the same mold and even more solidly. The activist is quite likely to be the person who will be most rankled by the pressures of the school's social system upon him and upon other newcomers. He is most likely to be the one who will rebel against the system's rules and expectations, quickly making himself unwelcome. Some returning Peace Corps volunteers have no doubt found this to be the case; others, however, have found ways to live within the system and to press for innovation.

Achieving innovation requires many skills, as well as patience. One of the key strategies among activists for baiting the "enemy" is that of confrontation. Activists are likely to find an issue and then demand an immediate cessation of its causal factors. That they may have a legitimate grievance is not relevant here. Any activist who indeed wants to make his impact on the schools from *within* must learn the ways of the system, its chains of command, and what points within the system will yield to change. Because the number of activists within school systems is very small, their chances of succeeding are generally rather slim. Confrontation is one strategy, but it generally results in a winner and a loser. Confrontation of a board of education, a superintendent, a principal, or a group of teachers, therefore, should occur only when other strategies have failed and only if the activist is prepared to risk losing. If his broader goal is to achieve as much change as possible, realizing that some battles must be lost, the activist will reserve confrontation for only the most serious situations, rather than using it as a general *modus operandi*.

As it is not likely that activists will be attracted to education, many will be involved in civil-rights groups and other groups that seek to implement change in the schools from without. Here again, if teachers are aware of the kinds of help they can receive from such activist

groups, a new *rapprochement* between civil-rights people and school people may be established. As things
stand now, there is an antagonism between those pressing for desirable changes from without and those within
the system who may see change as desirable but feel
threatened by the outsiders. Schools of education must
establish programs that are designed to recruit and to
train more and more activist students for teaching. This
training would in some ways have to be different from
that given other students in colleges of education. The
activists would demand the best faculty that schools of
education could offer and far more freedom in the types
of experiences designed to prepare them for their tasks.
Freedom does not mean that they would be sent into
the classroom without mastering the fundamental skills
that all teachers must have. It also does not mean that
all the students who are labeled "activists" on campus
are destined to be teachers. We are only suggesting that
the need for activists and innovators in the schools is
tremendous. Too many of these young people will never
enter education. Unless universities devise programs to
attract activists, programs that will focus on the difficulties of achieving change within the system, we shall
continue to lose their good services. The activist must
be fairly warned that he is unlikely to find great support
for his ideas in the school system if his only strategy is
that of confrontation. If he has alternative strategies,
his odds for survival and success are greatly increased. In
addition to teaching skills, activists must carefully map
out the types of strategies that they could utilize in
working with small groups of teachers, within teacher's

organizations, and with children to help bring about reforms in both the curricular and organizational patterns of schools.

Four Strategies

We accept as a premise that learning to become a teacher is not an easy task. We have not touched on the many types of skills and attitudes that an effective teacher must internalize. A good teacher not only must have skills in organizing materials, motivating children, managing children, and evaluating their progress but he also must be able to make professional decisions. He must know when to apply a skill, at what cost, and for which anticipated results. Such statements are easy to write, but their implementation requires specialized training. We must constantly challenge the strong sentiment that much of teaching is an art, or that good teaching boils down to a teacher's personality. That personality is a variable is unquestioned; but it is only one of many variables that produce a good teacher. Personality is in itself a variable that is affected by others. Although the debate regarding personality will be tempered by a growing body of research on teacher effectiveness, the controversy over whether or not teaching is an art will go on and on. We opt for the position well stated by Charles Silberman:

> To be sure, teaching—like the practice of medicine—is very much an art, which is to say, it calls for the exercise of talent and creativity. But like medicine, it is also—or

should be—a science, for it involves a repertoire of techniques, procedures, and skills that can be systematically studied and described, and therefore transmitted and improved. The great teacher, like the great doctor, is the one who adds creativity and inspiration to that basic repertoire. In large measure, the new interest in the development of electronic teaching technologies stems from the growing conviction that the process of instruction, no less than the process of learning, is in fact susceptible to systematic study and improvement.[7]

Teacher training will both gain prestige and make a vital contribution to public education when it focuses more sharply on the processes of instruction and learning. Some will argue that it already does fulfill this requirement, but we are not of this persuasion. Teachers must leave a school of education with the confidence that they have been exposed to and have *implemented* the best knowledge available about teaching and learning. And the implementation must be at a higher level of sophistication and intensity than it is now. At present, too much is learned at only a verbal, once-over-lightly level. In other words, if the anology fits, we would prefer a surgeon who has more than heard about a new technique; we would expect him to have practiced it many times before marking our abdomens. Similarly, well-prepared teachers must have experienced and practiced the newest and best techniques under a variety of settings, both theoretical and practical, before being licensed. Furthermore, those who cannot meet minimal standards should not be licensed, a step most teacher educators avoid with a passion. Educators continually point to the shortage of teachers when licensing standards are discussed, but this excuse has been used too long to cover up deeper problems.

Given all the variables that go into making a teacher effective, as well as the grid of convictions, prejudices, and experiences in each reader's background, we can submit four strategies that will reflect the basic premises of this work. The first of these is related to getting to know the community, the second to getting to know children, the third to becoming a student of pedagogy, and the fourth to becoming a student of the school as a social system.

STUDYING THE COMMUNITY We have already discussed the nature of a community study at length. It need only be restated that community studies are not simply accumulations of facts about given school communities. They should be systematic efforts to learn as much as possible about those segments of students' lives that are far more important in many ways than is the school day. Such a study calls for a teacher's commitment of time, energy, and intelligence. Many insights can be gained over a period of time through daily contact and conversations with children. But unless the teacher is willing to devote time to learning about the area in which he teaches, there is no reason to believe that the quality of his instruction will be in tune with the needs of his children. Once a teacher has undertaken several community studies, his future efforts will become less detailed. For the first time or two, there is no substitute for digging as deeply into the area as possible. If we are to break the tradition of teachers who are experts through the classroom window, the strategy of planning and implementing the community study must be one of the key skills covered in the training of the urban teacher. When parents in the area and community groups learn that teachers will come to them to *listen*, rather than to uplift, the teacher will know his community activities have been worthwhile. Only when that teacher feels that he can safely walk the streets of the area in which he teaches will he begin to become effective. As long as fear exists, it is pointless to elaborate on both the sociological and psychological implications of the situation.

GETTING TO KNOW CHILDREN Getting to know children has also been touched on in the section on the community study. Too often the idea of getting to know children receives only lip service in the form of admonitions to young teachers. We urge a concerted effort to get acquainted with one's students as rapidly as possible. Students, whatever their ages, whatever the subject, not only will readily discuss a wide variety of issues and ideas with teachers they trust, but also can help to make the teacher's efforts more realistic. Despite the pressures of mass education, a teacher who has been trained to utilize various questionnaire techniques, group-discussion techniques, small-group interviews, and individual interviews can in a short time gain a great deal of information from students regarding their likes and dislikes, their attitudes toward certain subjects, their feelings about how they are treated in school and out, their views on social problems, and a host of other matters. Armed with such knowledge, the teacher will less likely be satisfied with teaching the same old stuff in the same old way. Teachers who do not see the value of learning as much as they can about children will be less effective in reaching their children. We cannot predict that they will be completely ineffective, however, for many other factors contribute to effectiveness. The probability is that we shall have still another group of teachers who do not really care at all about their students. In our view, one way to evince caring for people is to listen to them and to learn from them. A teacher has a multitude of opportunities to listen. Even the newest neophyte can, if it is part of his teaching strategy, learn a great deal about his student body in a few weeks and can begin to plan accordingly.

A STUDENT OF PEDAGOGY   A third strategy is to become a student of pedagogy. By "pedagogy," a rather archaic word, we mean the skills of teaching. Unless a teacher develops a perspective on his own efforts, he will probably be one of the less effective teachers in the profession. Unfortunately, he will probably never know the difference. The range of competence tolerated in the profession is so wide that, as long as classes are orderly and forms are turned in on time, the quality of instruction is seldom analyzed. Only when a teacher recognizes the complexity of the subroles he must play and the skills he needs to encourage learning will he begin to look at his performance with some candor. We are not suggesting that teachers become coldly analytical, for it is unlikely that most of us can achieve this degree of detachment. We are suggesting that a teacher who examines his efforts regularly will not fall into the trap of blaming children if they do not learn, a rationalization heard over and over in schools. Experiences suggest that many of the wails and complaints about children who do not care or want to learn can often be traced to teachers who are unwilling to examine their own work.

Whatever the subject, whatever the technique, whatever the grade level, one's performance as a teacher is always open to improvement. The intricate dynamics of every classroom session offer many points for both positive and negative criticism, even in the best of classrooms. The teacher must supplement his own evaluation of his effectiveness if he is to move beyond the intuitive level. Talking to children, for example, is one way to gain insights. With older children, the utilization of anonymous questionnaires that deal with the teacher's performance is a useful tool. Some teachers even have the courage to invite colleagues to watch them teach, so that they can have an outside evaluation. The advent of portable television equipment will make such evaluations a part of teacher training in the near future; but, until that time arrives, many a teacher will have taught forty years and never once either heard his voice or seen himself in action. He has only the vaguest notion of what he does and whether or not he is effective. His eyes are constantly on his students and their reactions, but these indications are not necessarily accurate. In short, unless the teacher is willing to constantly examine his performance, there is little hope that he will be outstanding in his field.

A STUDENT OF THE SYSTEM A fourth and related strategy is to become a student of the system and of one's roles within it: the major theme of this book. Unless one rapidly learns how to survive within a school system, it is not likely that he will be an effective teacher. We are not suggesting that the neophyte teacher can spare either the time or the energy to study the school system as an anthropologist or a sociologist would. We are suggesting, however, that his training should stress various insights into the workings of the system, so that he can look at it realistically: taking an honest look at both the positive and negative aspects of teaching. The neophyte must learn that the roles he plays all have tolerances and that he has some leverage within which to operate. Obviously, he will need experience before he can truly become an innovator, an operator, or an intervener in the system. These terms are all value-laden, and some people will reject the concepts behind them. Again, we must stress that we are talking about teachers who are interested in doing the best they can for their children. If we can accept excellence as a common goal, then we should not be too concerned about terminology. For example, a real operator will quickly learn the methods and procedures for achieving a promotion within a system. Assuming that he has a modicum of aptitudes or skills required for promotion, the operator can ensure that he will be promoted over the so-called "good guy," who simply lets the fates determine his station. We suggest to the good guy that he also learn how to operate, both for his own sake and for that of his kids.

Be that as it may, we are concerned that the majority of teachers entering a system are overpowered by it.

They are staggered by the masses of children, by the power of administrators, by the debates on who should lead the profession, by community pressures upon the schools, by the financial crises facing schools, by the skills that must be developed all too quickly, by the inadequacy of many materials in use, by the fact that bells ring and children and teachers both respond with Pavlovian regularity, by the amount of energy drained day in and day out, by teaching conditions that are often substandard, by peers representing a range from true competence to sheer incompetence—all of these factors merge to form a confusing kaleidoscope to the newcomer. If the neophyte understands the workings of the system before entering it, the likelihood of his being able to handle its pressures and to master its demands in a short period of time is enhanced.

What we are saying of teaching may also be said of other complex social organizations, be it the church, the army, or a hospital. All these institutions demand professionals with certain skills. Among these skills is the ability to make professional decisions within the restrictions set by the system. Because teaching is a massive enterprise, a tradition has developed whereby teachers are essentially people who carry out orders. Such a tradition is not conducive to introspection. Very little training in the behavioral sciences is included in the preparation of teachers. Aside from the usual courses in educational psychology and perhaps a social foundations course or two, most teachers have not been prepared to be students of their own profession. We are not suggesting that courses alone can prepare teachers to

handle the vagaries of the system. But it is essential that
schools of education offer courses, laboratory experiences, and on-the-job internships that will prepare the
neophyte for his new career. If the neophyte is both
well trained and willing to be a constant student of his
profession, he will undoubtedly be a more effective
teacher. In short, we need, the type of teachers and
teacher-training institutions that will refocus their
efforts in the directions suggested by Warner Bloomberg:

> Even today the great majority of relevant research com-
> ing out of schools of education focuses upon the charac-
> ter of the child, his family, and his milieu as variables
> that prevent him from fitting in adequately with the
> ways in which his teachers and their administrators are
> prepared to conduct the educational enterprise. Where
> are the studies of the teachers and administrators who
> fail? Why haven't we an escalating inquiry into the
> character of school personnel, their families, and their
> cultural and social milieu as variables which prevent
> them from developing and carrying out effective means
> of engaging in a teaching-learning relationship with per-
> haps a third of our nation's children? Such research as
> we have tends to be biased in its formulation to protect
> what most professional educators prefer to take as the
> "givens." We emphasize curriculum and materials rather
> than teachers and children; or we focus on classroom
> techniques instead of the whole organization and cul-
> ture of the school; or we struggle to develop culturally
> unbiased tests to be distributed by teachers who suffer
> culture shock every time they walk into their classrooms.
> Again, most studies of successful administrators take in-
> ternal staff relationships as the dependent variable that
> is an index of success, failing to see that administrators
> and teachers can get along beautifully in sustaining in-

each other's contribution *to an educationally dysfunc-
tional organization and conduct of the teaching effort*.[8]

Many other strategies can be suggested, but we shall
not attempt to develop a typology or an ideal type of
teacher at this juncture. It is possible to do so, of course,
but the ideal type has been implicit in all that has been
written so far, and another few paragraphs will not
make him any more real. We can only stress that recruiting and training the "new breed" is impossible unless school systems permit a greater latitude of professional behavior than they do now. It only remains then
to focus on the "challenge of the times." It has become
popular to say that education no longer has problems,
only challenges. Perhaps there is a distinction, but we
have no preference for one or the other term. The problems or challenges facing urban education are very real,
but they are not necessarily new. Even the disadvantaged child is not a creature of this decade. He has been
a neglected client of every public school since the
masses of immigrants arrived on our shores. Since this
nation became committed to mass education and the
gamut of social classes became represented in the
schools, there has been a tremendous need for programs
and efforts to educate those children who are outside
the mainstream of American life. As we have noted, it
was only in the 1960s that the majority of educators
finally awakened to this fact and began to beat the
drum. Some educators recognized these needs and have
been beating the drum for generations; now their efforts
seem to be bearing some fruit. But the fruit will wither

unless a growing number of teachers is better equipped
and trained by preservice and in-service courses to work
with children in our urban schools. Our effort toward
this end has mainly been to outline the press of the
school's social system on the teacher. Our work is
merely an introduction. It has outlined and sketched
some dimensions and ignored others. Its value will be in
interesting some students of education to dig more
deeply into its suggestions.

What We Have *Not* Said

In bringing this discussion to an end, the basic theme
of the book may be best underscored by stressing what
has *not* been said. Such a back-handed approach is appropriate, as a number of negative aspects of teaching in
urban schools have been stressed. Whatever else the
reader may find within these pages, there are five major
points that are *not* basic to the theme, either explicitly
or implicitly.

First, the school system is not necessarily an enemy.
Despite its very rigid structure and its tremendous pressures toward standardization, opportunities exist within
every major school system for teachers and administrators to work toward innovation. America's system of
free public education is one of the great experiments in
democracy. It may deserve criticism, but it also needs all
the help it can get. Whatever its defects, it has contributed more to the evolution of democracy in our nation
than has any other single institution. Even its most severe critics are usually its products. It has been our in-

tent to stress how to survive within and change the system, rather than to urge its destruction.

Second, we have not attempted to blame the schools' problems on administrators or "downtown," as many educators do. Not that there are no incompetent administrators, for there are indeed too many who have retired on the job. Nonetheless, we have not offered administrators as scapegoats. Although one might wish that administrative positions and qualities of leadership were closely aligned, too often the opposite is true. In any large school system there are all kinds of administrators. It is up to the new teacher to size up his superiors and to seek out those who are open and supportive and to avoid or confront those who are closed-minded and timid. Happily, there is some small evidence that administrators will be held more and more accountable for their area of responsibility. Significantly, these demands come from outside the system, as do most other pressures for reform. It is anticipated that some principals will be demoted if their schools are not doing a good job of educating children. Although they have their problems, the buck must stop somewhere, and their role is critical to what a faculty does or does not accomplish. Demotion and other sanctions must be more frequently applied. The number of "educational leaders" who are entrenched in sinecures is simply too great. The same accountability, of course, must be applied to all people involved in public education, including teachers and college professors. By the same token, effective leaders need to be given the autonomy necessary to break through the bureaucratic morass.

Third, our discussion is in no sense an attack on teachers. I have worked with too many dedicated, hard-working individuals to fall for the usual claptrap that "teachers just don't care," as if all teachers were of this ilk. Given the very rigid and restricted framework within which most teachers must operate, it is a wonder that so many teachers survive as well as they do. We have stressed throughout that there is a tremendous range in the competence, commitment, and drive of teachers. No attempt has been made to gloss over the incompetents that are found in every major school system. But credit must also be given to those teachers who are doing good jobs under trying conditions. There are not enough good teachers to drive out the bad, however. On the contrary, Gresham's Law may be operative, and just the opposite is the case in some schools. Perhaps as professional organizations more firmly establish their positions as collective bargainers with boards of education, they may finally develop the types of internal mechanisms for admission into the profession that will rid the ranks of the incompetents who are now retained for a number of reasons.

Fourth, there has been no attempt to play down the scope of problems facing inner-city schools. Despite the emphasis that schools are more alike than they are different, wherever they are located in metropolitan areas, the fact remains that many schools, particularly in the inner city, are essentially custodial institutions. Even within these schools, there will be teachers and administrators putting up a good fight under trying conditions. One should not jump to the conclusion that they are fighting their children or community. On the contrary, they are often fighting to gain some recognition from the heads of their departments that they need more staff and resources than do other schools in order to do a more effective job. Unfortunately, very few major school systems have yet decided that inequalities can begin to be resolved only with differential budgets and freedom to deviate from the usual curricula and organizational patterns.

Fifth, we have not been suggesting that anyone who fights the system or says that it is bureaucratic is neces sarily a good teacher or a desirable addition to the school system. Although good teaching may be defined in many ways and there is a range of acceptable compe- tence, the fact remains that there are minimal standards of teacher competence that each and every teacher must meet. That a person is all against the system and all for the kids does not necessarily mean that he is a good teacher. Being a good teacher calls for much more than just commitment to a cause. We have certainly not been saying that being a neophyte teacher is tanta mount to being well trained, perceptive, eager, or any other positive attribute. In a very perceptive article deal- ing with the supervision of teachers, Marcia Conlin and Martin Haberman state: "We assume (erroneously) that beginners are more amenable to change than expe- rienced teachers. (This usually means 'susceptible to di- rective influences.' What are beginners changing from?)" [9] The latter question is rhetorical, of course, but its implication is clear: Newcomers have a lot to learn. New teachers who want to charge the system and set it right will learn the hard way just what being an agent of change means. Our goal has been not to discourage them but to outline both the possibilities and obstacles in the system. We need all the "changers" we can get, and we must help to prepare them for the hard knocks ahead. We cannot afford many more losses.

What we *have* been saying in various ways is that the "school marm" is dead; long live the new urban teacher! Or, "Good-by, Mr. Chips," and this time we really mean it! Urban schools demand teachers who not only are competent in teaching skills but who also recognize that the role of the teacher is much broader than it was a decade ago. The problems facing youth in our society demand teachers who are flexible in what they teach, how they teach, and in their willingness to engage in out-of-classroom activities, which may make the difference for children caught in the inequities of our way of life. Anyone entering the urban schools in the major cities of our country has to want to be where the action is. For anyone seeking to escape from life, the school is the last place to go. Urban schools need people who are willing to become involved. Our goal has been to suggest some forms that this involvement can take.

One point should be very clear. There is a difference between being part of a system and joining the system. Teachers must question the system of which they are a part. That does not mean that the system is an enemy, but it does mean that one must be prepared to change the system when it fails to educate a growing number of children. The emphasis on *what is* in this volume is intended to encourage a consideration of *what could be*. The schools of America are mechanisms for implementing ritualistic organizational patterns, goals, and curricula. The teacher who is willing to struggle actively with ritualism is too seldom found in our classrooms. He is the type of teacher we must attract and encourage if reforms are to become more than ideals.

Exhortations to action are easy; facing the censure of the system is not. How one goes about challenging the system is part of the solution, and internal mechanisms for reform should certainly be exploited. Yet confrontations are inevitable, for there are some issues on which there can be no compromise. If the system in any way perpetuates white racism in its curriculum, grouping, or hiring policies, the system must be challenged. If it ignores or merely "processes" the demands of black and civil-rights groups seeking to end discriminatory practices, it must be challenged. If it closes ranks around principals or teachers who are not working toward quality education, it must be challenged. If it punishes teachers who seek to work with the community or who deal with controversial issues, it must be challenged. Confrontation will place one at odds with principals, fellow teachers, professors, supervisors, and "downtown"—and sometimes with one's friends and family. One must also be prepared for attacks from bigots who are blind to our racial and socioeconomic wounds. Each teacher will determine the degree to which he will become involved, but one conclusion is inescapable. Our schools need teachers who are willing to pay the true price of professionalism, who have the will to fight their own system when it is wrong.

We shall not achieve an open society without a struggle. That same struggle must be undertaken in the schools. Our system of public education is worth fighting for. But the fight cannot be won unless teachers are willing to challenge the system from within.

Notes

1. *Cf.* Myron Lieberman, *The Future of Public Education* (Chicago: University of Chicago Press, 1960).
2. Frank Riessman and Arthur Pearl, *New Careers for the Poor: The Nonprofessional in Human Services* (New York: Free Press, 1965).
3. Charles E. Silberman, "Technology Is Knocking at the Schoolhouse Door," *Fortune*, (August 1966), 120–5.
4. Riessman, "Integration: The Key to Quality Education for All" (Address at the Symposium on School Integration, Michigan State University, May 1964).
5. Abraham Bernstein, *The Education of Urban Populations* (New York: Random House, 1967), p. 68.
6. Christopher Jencks, "Education: The Racial Gap," *New Republic*, 55 (October 1, 1966), 1–4.
7. Silberman, *op. cit.*, p. 124.
8. Warner Bloomberg, Jr., "Making the Urban School of Education Relevant," (Address at Conference on the Role of Urban Schools of Education, University of Wisconsin, Milwaukee, April 24–26, 1966). Italics added.
9. Marcia R. Conlin and Martin Haberman, "Supervising Teachers of the Disadvantaged," *Educational Leadership*, 24 (February 1967), p. 396.

A Note on Readings

Despite a deep respect for intellectual accomplishment and a love for books, we cannot go about listing all the works on the urban school, the inner-city school, and the disadvantaged child that have been published in the last two or three years. It is not because the list is too long but because of a conviction that secondary sources *must* be supplemented by first-hand experience and data. The value problems associated with urban schools are so intense that "words, words, words" are a necessary but not sufficient guide to understanding. If one is willing to become engaged in a first-hand analysis of the structure, function, and problems of the urban school and if one is prepared to listen to and observe children and teachers, the complexity and impact of what the phrase "urban schools" really means will be perceived. The following sources have helped me, and I recommend them as a starter.

Frank Riessman's *The Culturally Deprived Child* started the avalanche of books in the field and remains a key source. Riessman's role as an outspoken champion of the disadvantaged is not popular among all educators, but his impact is great, and his words deserve careful attention. Patricia Sexton's *Education and Income* is another must. Her documentation of inequities in school programs is often noted in demands for *unequal* allocations of resources if *equality* of education is to be achieved.

Paul Goodman's *Growing Up Absurd* and *Compulsary Mis-education* challenge the very structure and purposes of American education, and his ideas demand attention. John Holt's *How Children Fail* focuses on classroom activities and is a most revealing analysis of what actually goes on in classrooms day after day as teachers "ask" and children "recite." Any work by Edgar Z. Friedenberg is almost guaranteed to challenge one's thinking.

A subscription to the journal *Integrated Education* will introduce the new teacher to some of the more outspoken leaders in efforts to integrate schools. The *Urban Review* is another good source of candid reporting and opinion. Although education is only one of their interests, *The Nation, The New Republic,* and *Saturday Review* can be counted on for thought-provoking articles on the urban school. *This Magazine Is About Schools*, published in Toronto, is an example of the type of fresh thinking teachers need to consult if they are to be turned on.

Relevant to getting acquainted with life in urban schools, we noted several works in Chapter 1. For example, G. Alexander Moore's *Urban School Days* and Mary Green and Orletta Ryan's *The Schoolchildren* are appropriate and revealing sources. They are very different in approach, however; the former being systematic and the latter being impressionistic. Together they offer a realistic introduction. Bel Kaufman's *Up The Down Staircase* is certainly a pleasant way to be introduced to many of the nuances of life in the system. The National Education Association is also to be congratulated for *The Real World of the Beginning Teacher*, which touches on some of the ideas in the present work. It represents belated recognition from this organization that teaching is a tough job almost everywhere. *The Inner-City Classroom: Teacher Behaviors*, edited by Robert Strom, is still another good introduction to the field. Although I have some reservations about Jenny Gray's *The Teacher's Survival Guide*, particularly the stereotyping of disadvantaged youth, this slim, off-the-cuff book is a must for the new teacher. One need not agree with the techniques discussed in order to appreciate the candor of the approach.

For those interested in the sociological dimensions of school systems, Ronald Corwin's *A Sociology of Education* is highly recommended. It is especially useful for its analysis of the bureaucratic structure of education. And for the best single introduction to the facts of life in teaching, Willard Waller's *The Sociology of Teaching* is still without peer. Albeit dated, Waller's work is the inspiration for the present work, and his efforts remain a classic in the field.

We have not noted works by Kenneth Clark, A. Harry Passow, Nat Hentoff, Jonathan Kozol, Harry Rivlin, Robert Havighurst, and many others who are very current in urban school literature only because the above recommendations are intended merely to whet the appetite. Given a good grounding in this literature, the new teacher will be better prepared to undertake his own analysis.